Each New Day

Meditations During Challenging Times

Ken Nyhusmoen

Each New Day: Meditations During Challenging Times

Published by Wheatmark®
2030 East Speedway Boulevard, Suite 106
Tucson, Arizona 85719 USA
www.wheatmark.com

ISBN: 978-1-62787-891-3 (paperback)
ISBN: 978-1-62787-892-0 (ebook)
LCCN: 2021912027

Bulk ordering discounts are available through Wheatmark, Inc.
For more information, email orders@wheatmark.com
or call 1-888-934-0888.

Scripture references are from the Good News Bible, Today's English Version

Circa 1976

This book is dedicated to our children,
Karl, Andrea, and Philip,
who shared their lives
with the ministry of the church,
which was not an easy task.

INTRODUCTION

Beginning in March of 2020 we found ourselves in a time of isolation, confusion and some fear as we faced the Coronavirus pandamic. These devotional thoughts began as an avenue to connect with people who were often living alone in the retirement community of Green Valley, Arizona, and received communications from Desert Hills Lutheran Church. The writings continued until April, 2021 and a vaccine brought some relief from the fears of the Coronavirus.

The online messages were passed on to family and friends throughout the nation and our world. It appeared that these words of hope and encouragement brought some comfort to many people.

Through years of pastoral care I have discovered that throughout much of our lives we find ourselves feeling alone or afraid. It is my hope that this book of hope may provide that encouragement whenever life is a struggle.

As you read these words I ask that you keep in your prayers the families and friends of the almost 600,000 lives lost to this pandemic.

I am so grateful for the skilled editing and advice of my wife, Susan. Without her this book would never have been possible.

Pastor Ken Nyhusmoen

Hope in These Days

Paul, in his first letter to the Thessalonians, writes . . . "The hope of salvation is the helmet." (5:8)

I thought of those words today as I struggled with what message to share with you, my friends. A helmet is an article of protection . . . in football, most all sports . . . and in battle. Our grandchildren learned early that if they were to ride their bikes . . . dad and mom insisted that they wear a helmet.

Paul also tells us about how Hope is fashioned. "Not only so, but we also rejoice in our sufferings; because we know that suffering produces perseverance; perseverance, character; and character . . . Hope.

If you're like me, you're probably wishing there was a helmet somewhere that we could just 'put on' to protect us from these present times. Suffering is something we really try to avoid. But it usually comes to us someday . . . in one form or another.

We can endure just about anything if we have hope. Without it, we cannot survive. Let these words enter your spirit and your soul these days . . . "God is our refuge and strength, a very present help in time of trouble. Therefore, we shall not fear." "Come to me, those of you who are burdened and heavy laden . . . I will give you rest and peace."

Nothing can separate us from God's love. You are more than conquerors through God. Wear that hat! It is your helmet of salvation.

Wash your hands, fold them, bow your head and pray for protection.

God's peace . . . . where there is Hope . . . there is life.

Pray with me: Father, in these times, shelter us with your helmet of salvation and saving grace. Amen . . . in Jesus name, Amen.

We awoke this morning to a beautiful sunrise! I thought of the words . . . "The sun warms the earth, and the earth awakens".

In our home, we are 'hunkered down' . . . we have many projects and plans for the day. It's a 'new normal', isn't it? And yet . . . we know that all is not well . . . all is not secure.

Paul writes, "I have been in danger from rivers, in danger at sea, etc. And I have labored and toiled and have often gone without sleep; I have known hunger and thirst and have often gone without food; I have been cold and naked . . . Besides everything else, I face daily the pressure of my concern for all the churches." (2 Cor. 11:24-28)

Paul saw faith . . . not as something to prevent bad times, but as a shield, a kind of 'umbrella' that would keep bad times from doing him harm.

As I wrote of that helmet of protection the other day . . . today I'm thinking of an umbrella to tuck myself . . . and those I care about beneath . . . to keep us from all that appears to be raining down upon us.

Paul also wrote in Philippians . . . "I have learned to be content whatever the circumstances. I know what it is to be in need, and I know what it is to have plenty . . . . I have learned the secret of being content in any and all situations . . . I can do everything through him who strengthens me."

Let us look for contentment in our present situations today. We are together in this . . . do not feel alone. Come and tuck yourself in under that umbrella of faith.

Wash your hands, fold them and bow your head. Pray for some understanding.

Pray with me: "Dear Lord, let me find peace in my present situation . . . remove all fear and mistrust. Wrap your arms around me and grant me peace. In Jesus's name . . . Amen"

"The Lord is my light and my salvation – whom shall I fear?" (Psalm 27:1)

That's a strong message for us today. Security . . . or salvation . . . comes from God.

When I feel a bit insecure, as most of us do these days . . . I just want to crawl under the covers and block it all out! How about you? I find myself searching for the security blanket little Linus in Peanuts always carried around with him. Sometimes that blanket looked a bit dingy, dirty . . . but still Linus held on to it tightly!

What's our security blanket these days? Our security comes freely from God. And God is not like Snoopy . . . who would grab hold of that blanket and pull it away from Linus! Our security may feel like it's being pulled away from us. But it is definitely NOT.

God is not out there . . . somewhere . . . popping in and out of our lives. God is not distant in these present days.

God is with us. Within us. Within our church. God is in control. God is our light in darkness . . . our salvation in despair. We have nothing to fear.

I want to wrap that secure blanket around me . . . around my family . . . around my friends and neighbors . . . and around the church. That salvation from our loving God is my security blanket.

The stock market may fluctuate, up and down . . . the Coronavirus numbers may continue to rise . . . and yet, I know that

God is with us. Each and everyone of us. His blanket is wrapped completely around us and we are enveloped in His love.

Wash your hands, fold them and bow your head. Know that we are securely enveloped in the love of God.

Pray with me: "Dear Lord, be present today. Be with us in our waking and in our sleeping. Be with us in our loneliness and in our fear. Be with us each and every moment. Be with us, Lord , as we pray all these thoughts in Jesus' name. " AMEN

A thought for this day from Joshua 1:9 . . . "Have I not command-ed you? Be strong and courageous; do not be terrified; do not be discouraged, for the Lord your God will be with you wherever you go." And the beloved verse from Matthew 28:20 . . . "Surely I will be with you always, to the very end of the age."

That sounds nice, doesn't it? But as I have spent the past days speaking with many of you who are alone in your homes, or in your nursing home rooms . . . being strong and coura-geous is difficult, isn't it?

Take time to pray. Prayer is the way God makes himself aware to us. And we are not alone. Call upon God . . . and just start talking. It's actually very easy. Open your heart to Him and you will most certainly feel His presence. He is right there with you.

We had hoped to make a trip next month up to Minnesota to see the kids and grand kids. Our oldest granddaughter has a 'big' birthday (13) coming up and we most certainly want to celebrate it with her. In the far reaches of my mind I have such hope that we will be able to do that. But it doesn't look very promising right now. That is heartbreaking. I pray each day that we will all remain well so that those occasions can be enjoyed together someday.

For many people in our world right now . . . the future seems very bleak . . . scary. Look to scripture, folks. God has not deserted us. Jesus is on His Lenten Walk, He is lifting His cross over us. He walks alongside us as we can barely lift our feet to move forward.

"Do not be discouraged – or terrified. Be strong and courageous."

Stay well. Stay home. Wash your hands . . . and when you have finished . . .

Fold your hands . . . Bow your head. Give thanks.

God is Good . . . and He is right beside you.

Pray with me: "Dear Lord, fill us with your spirit, warm us with your love, give us peace as we place all our worries, our concerns in your open hands." Amen.

I have been doing quite a bit of reading lately . . . as well as many of you, I would imagine. It's kind of nice to have the time, and the solitude, to do that, isn't it?

I was reading an article about some mountain climbers. Upon reaching the summit, they were asked just what was it that kept them going on this arduous climb. They all answered the same way . . . " We knew the guy ahead was counting on us.. and we knew the guy behind needed us. We just had to keep on going. We promised each other."

As I thought about that article I was reminded of the verse from Isaiah 42:16

> . . . "I will lead my blind people by roads they have never traveled. I will turn their darkness into light and make rough country smooth before them. These are my promises, and I will keep them without fail."

We're all experiencing a bit of blindness as we travel down this rocky path right now. For most of us, this is a road we have never traveled. It seems awfully dark to me . . . maybe to you, as well. But it is God in Jesus Christ, as Rev. Dennis Nelson reminds us in our Lenten journey . . . who walks before us. He has the flashlight. He is walking ahead, helping us over the rough spots.

I'm depending on Him to hold me tight. I'm certain that you are, too. Keep a tight hold on that rope of faith. We may be lonely at times . . . but we are never alone. His promises are true. And as He says . . . . "I will keep them without fail."

Remember . . . wash your hands. Then fold them. Bow your head. Give thanks.

We're going to get through this time.

Pray with me: "Dear Lord, hold us fast. Hold us tight. Keep each of us and your church bound together during these days. We ask for strength for all who are tired, all who care for the sick, all who suffer. We pray especially now for your church. Help us to be the tight rope for those who reach out . . . and for those who simply need us. In Jesus' Name,

Amen.

TUESDAY, MARCH 31, 2020

From II Corinthians 4:17-18: "And this small and temporary trouble we suffer will bring us tremendous and eternal glory, much greater than the trouble. For we fix our attention, not on things that are seen, but on things that are unseen. What can be seen lasts only for a time, but what cannot be seen lasts forever."

As I have visited with many of you over the past days, I hear, again and again . . . "Why is this happening, Pastor Ken? I just don't understand."

Well, folks. I don't understand it either. There is so much of life that I fail to understand. I don't understand cancer . . . I don't understand the death of a newborn . . . I don't understand boys drowning in a lake while on a fishing trip. I don't understand ALS . . . I don't understand a young woman taking her own life.

Matter of fact. There's a lot I just DON'T GET. And I surely . . . do not understand this virus taking the lives of thousands of people.

But I do understand the words from Paul as he wrote to the Corinthians. I understand that this is a 'temporary' trouble. And I understand that God is very much with us during this trouble. I understand that His Great Love is being active with neighbors helping neighbors . . . with phone calls of encouragement and care. And I understand that medical and first responders are showing such dedication and commitment.

And dear friends . . . I fully and completely understand that we will go through this valley of the shadow . . . and we will come out on the other side. Remember . . . "What cannot be seen, lasts forever." His love is with us every day, every step of the way. And "May the Peace that passes ALL Understanding be with you all."

Pray with me: "Dear Lord, help us when we 'just don't get it'. Send your healing power to all who suffer, send the strength of your Spirit to all who are tired and weary. Send us some sense of understanding, dear Lord. In Jesus' Name. Amen.

Wash your hands. And then fold them, bow your head. Give thanks.

THURSDAY, APRIL 2, 2020

I've been going through some old photos and I found one from a Bible Camp in North Dakota taken around 60+ years ago. It brought back memories of sitting around the campfire at night and singing one song in particular . . . *"Have Thine Own Way, Lord . . . Have Thine Own Way. You are the Potter, I am the clay."*

We had an art activity at that camp and I remember struggling to make a pot. I'm no artist . . . and certainly, no potter! I remember throwing it down and then picking up the lump of clay and starting all over again. I don't remember the finished product very well, but I do recall it sitting upon my mother's windowsill for years.

That memory took me to Jeremiah 18:3 . . . *"So I went there and saw the potter working at the wheel. Whenever a piece of pottery turned out imperfect, he would take the clay and make it into something else."*

I wonder if that is something God is doing with us these days. Maybe as we are compelled to 'stay at home', God is making us into something new. Maybe God is in the process of creating something a little bit stronger . . . or more loving . . . more caring . . . even more generous.

I also wonder if when we emerge from our homes and these troubling times we may see our own selves a little differently. The Potter is hard at work within us. He is forming us, always creating something new in us. Let us find ourselves a bit more pliable as He forms and fills and creates a new spirit within us.

Remember . . . Wash your hands! Fold them, bow your head and let the Potter do His creative work!

Pray with me: "Dear Lord . . . You are, indeed, the Potter. We are but a lump of clay. Mold us and make us into a new creation, ready to do Your work in the world . . . to make a Difference. And as you are at work forming and making us, we ask for your strength and courage for all those who care for the sick and dying. Give them power to carry on."

Amen. In Jesus' Name . . . Amen

SATURDAY, APRIL 4, 2020

It's very strange to be heading into Holy Week this way, isn't it? After walking the Lenten walk on the way to the cross we don't find ourselves by the side of the road, waving palms and cheering . . . "Hosanna!"

No . . . here we are. "Hunkered down . . . staying home." Personally, I will go out and cut a palm branch from one of our palm trees in our yard. I'll lay it on the dining room table. It will become our centerpiece as we journey that final trip to the cross this week.

There is always something just so wonderful about the opening of our Palm Sunday worship services . . . we stand and sing loud and clear . . . "Hosanna to the King of Kings!" Here He comes! Just as is promised each and every year. At the end of those six weeks of Lent we can finally rise up and give Him the honor He deserves!

Well . . . we can still do that. He's still coming to us. We may not be in one another's 'presence' . . . but we most assuredly are in HIS PRESENCE. We'll still be right there . . . on the sidelines, greeting the King of Kings as He make His way through this next week.

They say . . . "Absence makes the heart grow fonder". I think that is very true for me right now, and perhaps, for you. I'll miss sharing this week with my co-workers, my fellow church members, etc. But we will still be together. Because we have a bond that cannot be broken by 'absence'. We are very much in each other's presence . . . because we are held together by the ever present, omnipotent King of Kings. And He is with us as we journey our final way to the cross this week.

May God bless your walk . . . we'll be together in worship . . . 'online'. Nothing can separate us from the love of God in Christ Jesus.

I remind you to wash your hands, fold them . . . bow your head. Give thanks for the 'presence' that passes all our understanding.

Pray with me: "Dear Lord, we worship and adore you . . . we ask for your help these days. Give strength to all as we journey together to the cross. Amen. In Jesus' Name, Amen.

A thought for today . . . "So do not worry about tomorrow; it will have enough worries of its own. There is no need to add to the troubles each day brings." (Matthew 6:34)

I have had the habit for years of making a 'To Do' list. Each morning I usually take out a slip of paper and write on it all the things I think I need to accomplish that day. These past days I have found that my list is totally blank. Oh, yes . . . I still have plenty to do! I have enjoyed many phone conversations with many of our members as we have passed through this time. That's my main . . . To Do. But I don't need to write down . . . "Call on the phone!" I pretty much know that's what I will do each day.

We rise early . . . often enjoying the sunrise. We go to bed early . . . earlier than we used to! And each day passes . . . there is a lot to worry about but I'm trying to make myself more and more aware of this passage from Matthew . . . "Do not worry about tomorrow".

Years ago I worked as a counselor with people struggling with substance and alcohol abuse at a treatment center in Northern Minnesota. Many of these folks had to keep telling themselves.."Just take it ONE DAY AT A TIME." Over and over . . . each and every day. That's kind of where we are right now. Just appreciating the sunrises and anticipating the sunsets . . . one day at a time.

And we know that God is in those moments. He is reminding us through scripture to take Monday . . . live it. Then take Tuesday . . . all the way through this week until the sun rises on

Easter Morning. "There is no need to add to the troubles each day brings."

Have strength for the journey this week we call Holy. Wash your hands, then fold them . . . bow your head . . . give thanks.

Pray with me: "Heavenly Father, through the suffering, death and resurrection of your Son, Jesus Christ you have empowered us to face our own journeys . . . our days . . . with your sustaining love. Strengthen all who are sick, and those who walk the front lines for us. Amen. In Jesus' Name, Amen.

APRIL 8, 2020

C.S. Lewis writes . . . "True humility is not thinking less of yourself, it is thinking of yourself less."

And in Philippians 4, verse 5 we read, "Show a gentle attitude toward everyone. The Lord is coming soon."

Maybe we are experiencing a 'kinder', 'gentler' time. I hope so. I read something written by one of our Green Valley neighbors urging us all to honor the 'social distancing' requirements, emphasizing what decisions we make do not only affect us . . . they affect others.

That is so true in all things, isn't it? Our reactions to one another at all times, but most certainly these days are so important. As we sit at home we may find ourselves thinking of 'just ourselves' . . . or we may be thinking *less* of ourselves and finding our thoughts wandering to others. Our families, our neighbors, our fellow church members.

We are hearing stories of the dedication and courage of so many health care workers, firefighters, police . . . social workers, grocery clerks, delivery people. The list goes on and on. Philippians reminds us as we walk the final steps to the cross . . . to show a gentler attitude to all people. And then we hear the words, "The Lord is coming soon". The same Jesus who met his followers at the table on Maundy Thursday and then hung upon the cross on Good Friday is definitely coming soon!

He is going to burst out of the tomb on Easter Morning. We know that to be true. These days are just a 'snipet' of time. The Lord is coming soon! Spend this week we call Holy to focus on

His Victory over death. Walk together, maybe not 'side by side' but most certainly TOGETHER as we journey on to Easter Day and the perfect assurance that God is in control.

Let us be gentle with one another.

Wash your hands, fold them. Bow your head . . . Give thanks.

Pray with me: "Dear Lord, strengthen us not to dwell so much on our own selves and our present situation . . . but upon others. We ask for courage for all during these days. And grant us the Peace . . . which passes all understanding . . . as we walk these days, with one another . . . to the cross. Amen, In Jesus' Name, Amen.

FRIDAY, APRIL 10, 2020

TODAY we walk with Jesus on the way to the cross. We stand beside him as the crown of thorns is placed upon his head. We watch as he is stripped of his clothes . . . spit at and mocked.

And then we see him led away. But on the road we encounter Simon of Cyrene. This one man is forced to shoulder the burden of the cross. (Mark 15:21) It's a large wooden cross, very heavy. He probably wasn't very eager to do it. But he did.

In our home we have a small piece of art. It's a cross being carried by many small children. They each shoulder a part of it. Perhaps many of you either have the same piece or something similar. We keep it out year round. But during Lent and Holy Week it holds a prominent place on our table.

That small statue reminds me that if these little children can carry the cross, most assuredly, I can bear it too. I remember the old hymn . . . "Must Jesus Bear the Cross Alone and all the world go free? No, there's a cross for everyone . . . and there's a cross for me."

This year it may seem like that cross is just a bit heavier than we would want it to be. But, much like Simon, we pick it up and carry our load.

It's a hard day . . . Good Friday. I feel weighed down, don't you? But unlike Simon . . . who walked that road with Jesus and carried the cross, we know the outcome! We know that it is just a small matter of time before we'll cry out . . . "He Is Risen!" It's just a matter of time before we'll leave our sheltered cave and burst out into full life once more.

Keep on washing your hands . . . fold them, bow your head. Give Thanks.

Pray with me: "Dear Father, into your hands we commend all that gives us pain, suffering, grief. Grant us strength for the walk. Give help to all in need, those who suffer and those who share the burden. Amen. In Jesus' Name, Amen.

APPY EASTER! How amazing it was to wake this morning for the sunrise and the possibility of a brand new day! I always like to say . . . "**WAKE UP! EASTER PEOPLE!**" Wake up to what is ahead . . . before us. It's like discovering a chance to start all over again. Easter does that for us!

Years ago in my first parish we had a young man named Donnie. As we would plan for our worship services with full choirs . . . full organ . . . traditional hymns, trumpet fanfare . . . Donnie would come to me and say . . . "Please may I sing 'Because He Lives'?"

Oh my. Sometimes it was a dilemma. The worship committee wasn't on board. But, of course . . . the answer was always YES. It's a gospel song that most of us find familiar.

"Because He lives . . . I can face tomorrow. Because He lives, all fear is gone. Because He lives, I know the future. And life is worth the living . . . just because He lives."

I can still close my eyes . . . and see him proudly standing before the congregation, his voice would waver a bit . . . not a particularly strong soloist . . . but the truth of that song carried this young man through many trials and finally, death . . . . and to life everlasting.

In Galatians 2:20, we read . . . "So that it is no longer I who live, but it is Christ who lives in me. This life that I live now, I live by faith in the Son of God, who gave his life for me."

So it is for us. Because He burst out of the tomb, we too shall rise! This grave could not hold Him . . . the Living Christ in whom we believe. And these present trials will not define us either. We have New Life! It's a New Day, Easter People! This is the most powerful message we will ever hear. We have another chance!

Because He lives . . . . I can face tomorrow. And so, can you . . . my friends.

Wash your hands. Fold them, bow your head. Give thanks. He LIVES!!

Pray with me: "Heavenly Father, we thank you for the gift of your Son, our Lord. Give us strength to face tomorrow because we know *He Lives*. Grant your healing presence on all who suffer, give courage to those who feel worn down. Amen, In Jesus' Name, Amen."

APRIL 16, 2020

So, here we are. Another day to 'stay at home'. I usually have a routine from which I very seldom waiver. Coffee, breakfast . . . shave and shower, dress up and head off to work. But I don't have to follow that every single day now. Some mornings I take quite a bit of time to 'get ready' for the day. Some mornings when I look in the mirror . . . I see myself, as I really am! **Not always that good**, to be honest.

These days have offered me a good amount of time for reflection. And I would imagine most of you have done the same. It's been a kind of spiritual 'cleansing' for me. I remember a gentleman from my first parish . . . we were having some conflicts in the church and he said one day . . . "Those people are just so spiritually minded they are no earthly good!" It's an old saying, I'm sure most of you have heard it before.

Wherever you are in your spiritual journey I challenge you to think about those words. Or maybe the reverse is true . . . some of us may be so 'earthly minded we are no spiritually good!"

Those thoughts took me to the 5th Chapter of Matthew . . . beginning with verse 3. We call these verses The Beatitudes. These words remind me of the simple truths of Jesus' teaching. Can we take these days, this time 'set apart' to think of this as an invitation to enter into a new approach to how we live? Maybe even to see ourselves in the mirror . . . "as we really are"? Perhaps this is one of those times when the **cracks** we are experiencing in life are really **opportunities** to let the light shine in.

I ask you to think about that . . . now, open your Bibles to Matthew 5 . . . read the Beatitudes. Good reading.

Wash you hands, fold them . . . bow your heads . . . give thanks.

Pray with me: "Dear Lord, inspire us to use these days of solitude to discover more deeply WHO we REALLY are. Help us to take a good look at ourselves and what it is we can do in our homes, our communities, our church, our world . . . to make a Difference. Amen. In Jesus' Name, Amen.

APRIL 18, 2020

From Romans 12:5 . . . *"In the same way, though we are many, we are one body in union with Christ, and we are all joined to each other as different parts of one body."*

I heard someone on TV speak about how important it is during this time to keep our connections alive. He said in prior days, he often put off going to his mother's home for coffee, or even calling her back as he was so consumed with work. These days . . . he would give anything to sit with his mother in her home and drink a cup of coffee.

It's so important for us to keep our 'connections' secure now . . . . and always. We may be physically separated . . . but we are all joined together. I am reminded of that when I enter the church sanctuary to record the liturgy for our worship services. Although the 'building' is empty, I feel the presence of all of you . . . and the angels and the archangels as we are joined together in worship.

I remember when we moved to Green Valley. Someone asked my wife . . . "How will you ever make new friends at this point in life?" We wondered about that, as well. And yet . . . here we are 7 years later. With many friends, great neighbors . . . and most of all, a loving church family. We cherish the bonds we have forged. We miss our family so much but we know that our connections are secure. We are all joined together as different parts of one great body.

Being joined together as friends and family often means allowing some space in our relationships. We don't all think alike . . . we don't all approach life the same . . . we are very different. And yet we are joined together. This is a time for us to find that common bond. Romans reminds us in this chapter very clearly that 'Love must be completely sincere' (vs 9).

It's a good chapter to read right now as we reflect upon our lives together and our lives in God's service. I especially like vs. 12:

Let your hope keep you joyful, be patient in your troubles, and pray at all times."

Concentrate on those words . . . JOYFUL . . . PATIENCE. And . . . don't forget to wash your hands, fold them . . . bow your head. Pray and give thanks for all these good 'connections'.

Pray with me: "Dear Lord, give us strength for our journeys, patience for what troubles we have and most of all . . . JOY in the warmth of your loving grace. Keep us close. Keep us connected. Grant healing to all who suffer, strength to those who keep on working even when they are weary. Amen. In Jesus' Name, Amen.

Don't you feel, as I do, that we are all on a kind of journey? The only problem is . . . our GPS is failing us and we find ourselves not sure where we are headed! And almost every day, I want to ask . . . **"Are we almost there???"**

I found myself reading Isaiah, and in chapter 58, vs. 11, I found some direction . . .

"And I will always guide you and satisfy you with good things. I will keep you strong and well. You will be like a garden that has plenty of water, like a spring of water that never goes dry."

I need those words as we face another week of 'Stay At Home'. No matter where we are headed . . . we have a guide, a real GPS! And He will keep us strong and well. No matter what physical or emotional fears come to us . . . we are fed and watered by his empowering love.

When we travel we tend to make a lot of stops. We'll pull off, here or there, take a break, capture a photo of a view or even read a monument. I feel that we are kind of doing that right now. We're on a road, but we find ourselves distracted by what it happening. We pull off. We become fearful or even lose some hope.

But then . . . we get 'On the Road Again' (just like Willie!) And the interesting thing about that is we don't go back to the beginning, do we? No, we pick up where we paused. Our faith keeps us focused once more and we go on our way. This time might just be a 'pause', a time for us to look at the view . . . gather all the facts . . . and then face forward with our guide right in front of us . . . leading and directing us to the final destination.

Read Isaiah . . . God's promises of hope and healing are clearly revealed. Not just for days past, but for our future. He made a covenant with his people. That covenant is for us, as well.

Enjoy your journey this week! It may hold a few surprises! Be sure to wash your hands, fold them . . . bow your head and give thanks for His direction.

Pray with me: "Dear Lord, just as you led your people centuries ago, lead us now. Be our strength and our guide. Keep us faced in the right direction. We ask for strength for all those who are parched and weary, and healing for those who suffer. Amen. In Jesus' Name,

Amen.

APRIL 22, 2020

It certainly is hard to practice 'self control' while *Staying At Home*, isn't it? We find ourselves talking about what's for dinner first thing in the morning! I would imagine, like many of you, there are way too many trips to the refrigerator throughout the day!

As I watch the numbers on the scale go up . . . I started thinking about Self Control. In Galatians chapter 5, vs. 22-23 we read:

> *"But the Spirit produces love, joy, peace, patience, kindness, goodness, faithfulness, humility, and self control. There is no law against such things as these."*

During this time when we have experienced more 'closeness' than usual, most of us may have had to think a little more about self control. Not only in the kitchen . . . but throughout the house! We used to tell our kids . . . "Interact, don't react!" Self control is a virtue, for sure. We can choose our reactions to all situations. Not just our present moment. When we are hurt, we often become resentful. When we feel that we have completely lost all control . . . we can still choose how to handle the situation.

This is a time when many emotions can run wild. Having very little control over what we do . . . where we go . . . is frustrating, for sure. This is a time when those words from the hymn really seem to take on a new meaning . . . *"Make me a captive, Lord and then I shall be free."*

It may be wise for us to dig deep and use this time and these experiences to focus on 'self control'. We will make it through this . . . and when we do, we will be grateful to have dug deep into ourselves to discover our forgiving spirit and . . . some self control.

Read Galatians . . . especially Chapter 5, beginning with verse 16. There's a lot in there about our human spirit. This is also a good time for us to focus on deeds of love and mercy. For it is in doing for others, caring for others . . . that we find a strength we didn't even know we had. And also . . . a bit of 'self control'.

Wash your hands . . . . fold them . . . bow your head and pray . . . give thanks.

Pray with me: "Heavenly Father, we reach out to you for courage for the day. We ask for strength for the moment. Help us to hold our tongue, think through our actions and put the needs of others before our own. Give healing to those who suffer with pain, give comfort to those who struggle with grief. And give us all a forgiving heart and a loving spirit. We ask this in the Name of Christ, our Lord. Amen. In Jesus' Name, Amen.

FRIDAY, APRIL 24, 2020

We are celebrating Easter! What? You may say . . . "Has he completely lost it? Easter is over!" Oh no . . . we are very much in the season of Easter and we continue to celebrate! We are Easter People!

That thought brought me back to Matthew, chapter 28. It's a story we love to read over and over again as we continue to celebrate Easter! I focus today on verse 19:

"Go then, to all peoples everywhere and make them my disciples: baptize them in the name of the Father, the Son, and the Holy Spirit . . . "

GO! Might that be what we are doing? The church is all about 'gathering' and yet . . . in this verse we are told to GO! In his book, *The Wonder of Being Loved*, Al Rogness writes a chapter he has entitled, "The Shattered Walls". In it, he says . . . "The church has two mandates. It is to bring the world into the church, and it is to bring the church into the world."

As I hear from many of you, maybe that is what is happening during this time. This may be a time to 'bring the church into the world'. You tell me how you are sharing our email messages and our worship services with friends and families all over the country, and the world. Even when we are sheltered in place we are compelled to share the Good News . . . to GO! And we can do that. It is our mission . . . Easter People . . . to not become complacent. To share the courage and the comfort we have received from our God with all people. So . . . continue to Celebrate Easter! Even from your own four walls. Tell everyone what He has done! Share the strength you have received from the Easter message with those you love . . . . and maybe with those you aren't so sure about!

Our church is On The Move! We are ONE together. Not within four walls, but within the structure and the form of our faith. Take it . . . . GO WITH IT! There is such Good News to talk about.

And while you're at it . . . don't forget to wash your hands. Fold them, bow your head and give thanks for the Easter message. He is Alive! He lives among us, right where we are. Right Now. Go back and read Matthew 28. Keep celebrating Easter!

Pray with me: "Dear Risen Lord, give us the courage to share the Good News. Just where we are. Give us the strength to reach out to all who stumble. We pray especially now for those who are sick, for those who care for the sick, for those who do the work that needs to be done during these days. Amen. In Jesus' Name, Amen.

I've been spending some time reading Matthew . . . especially the chapters that tell of the parables of Jesus. I like story telling. That's really what they are. Stories of what Jesus can do for us as we face our daily lives.

I especially like the one about Jesus Walking on the Water . . . Chapter 14:22-32. We lived on Lake May in northern Minnesota. The water doesn't warm up there very quickly in the Spring. Putting the dock out was always a test of courage for me. I would try so hard NOT to have to go into the water! I would think of Jesus and his message to Peter when Peter saw him coming to the fishermen on the top of the water. COME! Wouldn't it have been great to have the trust of Peter and just walk across the water? I'm pretty confident that no matter my degree of trust . . . I'd have fallen in.

But that's not really what the story is talking about . . . walking on water. It speaks to us of TRUST. Trust in the commands of Jesus. Believing Him when He tells us . . . "Your faith is strong! You have no need to doubt!"

It may be difficult to muster up that trust factor these days. Who do we trust? As I sat out on our patio this morning, the birds were just singing like crazy! Our world seemed so perfect . . . so beautiful. Bright blue sky, still a little cooler temp, bird songs. And I thought about trust. About trusting in our God so completely. Trusting in Him to come to us across the wild, rocky sea . . . and remind us of WHO is really in control.

"This is my Father's world, Oh, let me never forget. That, though the wrong seems oft so strong. God is the ruler yet. This is my Father's world; Why should my heart be sad? The Lord is King, let the heavens ring: God reigns, let the earth be glad!"

Difficult days? Yes. But dig deep inside and muster up that **Trust**. (And give some thought to reading those parables in Matthew).

Remember . . . wash your hands! Then fold them, bow your head. Give thanks . . . and Trust.

Pray with me: "Dear Lord, help us to trust you in all things. You, who can walk across the waves and reach out your hand to us on our stormy seas. We give you thanks. We ask now for courage for those who suffer, strength for those who minister. We pray for our church, the whole church. And we pray for our world. Amen. In Jesus' Name, Amen.

In Revelation 22:13, we read . . .

"I AM the first and the last, the beginning and the end."

Sometimes we hear it as . . . "I AM the ALPHA and the OMEGA . . . the beginning and the end."

We always like to make plans. (Not just about what to eat for dinner) . . . but plans as to what we would like to do next. In the fall . . . . 'we should . . . ', or next year . . . 'let's do . . . ' Just now we aren't really making too many concrete plans. We speak often of the 'beginning' of this stay at home life; we talk about what 'today' will bring. But we know very little about the ending.

When I'm reading a particularly exciting book, I may sneak a peak at the ending. I'm always disappointed when I do that. It kind of ruins the middle. So. Here we are. Stuck in the middle. The end may be near, but we aren't too sure about that.

What does Scripture tell us at this point? Well . . . not only in Revelation, but in many other places in the Bible we are reminded that God is in the Beginning. He is in the Middle. He will most assuredly be with us in the End.

Think for a moment about Jesus. He started on his journey and he asked the disciples to go along with him. They had no idea what the ending would be. They just picked up and followed in the beginning and stuck with him through the middle all the way to the end.

We are kind of like that right now. Stuck in the middle. Hoping for a good ending. No matter what comes our way we are like that original band of brothers. We're in this together. And being a part of the fellowship of believers . . . the church . . . OUR CHURCH . . . gives us faith to just keep trudging along. We can't peek ahead to see the end. We have no idea. No clue how this is all going to pan out. But we know we are not going through it alone . . . we TRUST.

"Yea . . . though I walk through the valley . . . . You are with me."

He was there in our beginning . . . washing us with our Baptismal waters. He has been there with us in our middle . . . through our lives every step of the way. And He is sure to be with us at our end. The end of this present trial, and the end we will some day face, which, actually . . . May be just a NEW BEGINNING!

Don't forget to wash your hands, fold them . . . bow your head. Give thanks to this great God who is always with us.

Pray with me: "Dear God . . . You are the great I AM. The Alpha and the Omega. The beginning and the end. And thankfully . . . You are the middle, as well. Amen. In Jesus' Name, Amen.

THURSDAY, APRIL 30, 2020

Have you ever used the term . . . "It is what it is"? I have. Some things you just can't change. They are what they are.

I remember when we moved to my first parish. It was in a very small town in ND and we had our own water well. One day we were visited by one of the older members of the church, he stopped by to drop off some eggs. He asked us how things were going and we mentioned that the water seemed very rusty. (it was awful, by the way). He calmly looked at us and said . . . "It is what it is."

In other words . . . 'get over it'. We laugh now when we think back about those days. Eventually, we got a new well and everything got better.

But I think of that today as I reflect upon Isaiah 14:24 . . . *"Surely, as I have planned, so it will be, and as I have purposed, so it will happen."*

Sometimes our acceptance of a present situation is difficult. We struggle with our loss of control . . . we like to feel we are always in charge. Giving up the power, that's difficult. But there are things that are just completely beyond our control. That's kind of where we find ourselves today.

It is what it is. Live with it. The strength we find in scripture . . . places like Isaiah help us to do just that. As we age, we often find ourselves a little more accepting to that thought. We've seen so much that has just been beyond our control that we realize we are not the ones calling the shots.

The Loving Kindness Prayer goes like this:

"As I grow older, may I be kind to myself; As I grow older, may I accept joy and sorrow; As I grow older, may I be happy and at peace."

This prayer might be a good option for us as we begin each day asking God for acceptance. It's just about trust, I guess. And that's a good thing.

Don't forget about washing your hands . . . fold them, have you ever noticed that your thumbs in folded hand position form a cross? . . . bow your head, give thanks. It is what it is.

Pray with me: Dear Lord, give us the strength to accept these things we cannot change. Amen. In Jesus' Name, Amen.

I'd like to ask you to read I Corinthians, chapter 12 when you have a moment. We were thinking the other day about 'spiritual gifts' and in this chapter Paul goes a little further as he writes, beginning in verse 12, about **'One Body with Many Parts'.**

I found myself reflecting on that as I thought of those many people who have struggled with physical pain and discomfort throughout this crisis. Not just those who have contracted the virus, but medical people with scars on their faces from the use of masks, first responders who have had to enter unknown territory at any moment. You can only imagine the pain some people have had to endure.

And some of you have struggled, as well. I speak on the phone with you and I hurt for what you have to endure. When one of us hurts . . . we all hurt.

Being a part of a church family is a big deal to me. Throughout my life as the ups and downs have occurred, it has been not only my immediate family that has given me love and support, it has been my church family. When one of us is hurt, physically or emotionally, we hurt for one another.

I have so much trouble with my feet! I constantly think I'm going to get on a serious physical workout program and then my head just hurts . . . because my feet hurt! Stub your little toe? Don't you almost feel faint? Bump your elbow? Wow! Felt that in my stomach!

It may be simplistic . . . but it is true. The body is ONE BODY. I see the church the same way. We are ONE BODY.

When one of us struggles, we struggle together. Because we are a part of this family we are here for one another.

> Vs. 18-19: "As it is, however, God put every different part in the body just as he wanted it to be. There would not be a body if it were all only one part! As it is, there are many parts but one body."

So . . . you are hurting. So am I. And I hurt for you. And I know that you hurt for me. But it is truly this ONE BODY who will get us through this time and times to come, together.

> Vs. 26: If one part of the body suffers, all the other parts suffer with it: If one part is praised, all the other parts share its happiness."

I cannot wait to worship with you this weekend. Isn't it amazing how we can all come TOGETHER . . . every part, ONE BODY? . . . Stay Connected!

Remember to wash your hands, fold them and bow your heads. One Body doing that together.

Pray with me: "Dear Father in heaven, continue to bind us together, mold us, make us . . . keep us ONE BODY. Amen, In Jesus' Name, Amen.

'Fiddler on the Roof' has always been one of my favorite musicals. We've seen it many times in different forms. My favorite song is "Sunrise, Sunset". *"Is this the little girl I carried? Is this the little boy at play?"* I think of that especially these days as we find ourselves a little lonesome for our children and our grandchildren. We know our grandchildren are growing so rapidly. Our oldest granddaughter just turned 13 last weekend. Unbelievable!

Sunrise . . . and then, Sunset. One day.

I get up very early and really like to watch the sun come up over the mountains. These days I think each morning of what the day may bring. I read somewhere . . . 'we are all born on one day, we die on one day, we can change on one day, we may fall in love on one day, anything can happen . . . on just one day'.

The Bible tells us a lot about living our lives day to day as we anticipate the end of time. In II Peter, chapter 3 vs. 8, we read, *"But do not forget one thing, my dear friends! There is no difference in the Lord's sight between one day and a thousand years, to him the two are the same."*

So each day we sit in darkness until the light comes. Some mornings it comes slowly and some mornings it just seems to explode. We have that day. One day. It's really a gift. Sunrise to sunset. We can chose to live it in any way. No matter what our present circumstance, it is given to us. Then the light goes to darkness. Think of that in comparison to our life here on earth.

One day is like a thousand years in God's sight. During these current days let us choose to live each day to the fullest. To reflect . . . to refresh . . . to renew. For this is but a fleeting moment. Really, it's just one day.

> *Psalm 90:4 . . . "A thousand years to you are like one day; they are like yesterday, already gone, like a short hour in the night."*

Don't forget about the washing your hands part, fold them, bow your head, give thanks for this wonderful day of Grace!

Pray with me: "Holy God, we give you thanks for each day you give us. We are grateful for the beautiful sunrises and the amazing sunsets. We rejoice for each moment we draw our breath. We ask for healing for those who suffer, those in pain. We ask for strength for caregivers and for those who are weary and worn down. And when we close our eyes tonight, lift our hearts and our minds to you. Amen. In Jesus' Name, Amen.

MAY 6, 2020

As I am writing these devotionals I find myself returning time and time again to the book of Isaiah. Maybe it's because we find ourselves in a situation where we, like the people of Judah, are in need of the constant reassurance that God does fulfill his promises.

Many years ago we had an old Volkswagen hatchback. It did not run well, and it certainly was no thing of beauty. That car would find the worst places to stall! I remember being behind the wheel and just wishing and hoping that as I pumped and pushed it would take off! The worst was when it would happen in front of the school as I dropped the kids off in the morning. EMBARRASSING!

Ever been like that old crate . . . in a stall? Just cannot get yourself to take off? Not really going backwards . . . but forward isn't working either.

Isaiah 43:19 reminds us when we find 'stuck' or 'stalled' in our faith, that the Lord is behind the wheel . . . "Watch for the new thing I am going to do. It is happening already – you can see it now! I will make a road through the wilderness and give you streams of water there."

I'm ready to get on the road. To put these days behind us. But we aren't the ones in control, are we? All we can do is follow the path . . . watch for the Lord . . . (wait on the Lord) and then He will direct us down that road. He will make a road through this wilderness and give us streams of water. Take some time to read Isaiah . . . it helps.

This weekend I will be sharing a sermon on "Patience". I

hope you take time to listen. I'm not very patient, maybe you aren't either. But the WORD helps us. It inspires us.

Wash your hands. Fold them. Bow your heads. And then wait for that road to be open to all of us.

Pray with me: "Dear Lord, give us patience when we find ourselves in a stall . . . when we feel 'stuck'. Help us to look to you for guidance as we head on down the road ahead. We pray for all who are sick, shut in, and especially for those who carry the heavy burdens on the road. Amen. In Jesus' Name, Amen.

In Mark, chapter 10, beginning with verse 17, we read of the rich man who came to Jesus asking him *"What must I do to inherit eternal life?"* Jesus looked straight at him and 'with love' said . . . *"You need to sell all you have and give the money to the poor."* The man became very sad, because he was really rich.

Give it up! Not easy for us either, is it? We've been doing quite a bit of that lately. Cleaning out the closets, the cupboards, sharing books with friends and neighbors. We've had some time to reflect on all that we have and also . . . all that we really don't need.

I was thinking about that and my thoughts turned from earthly things to what seems to clutter my mind. Some past grievances, some opinions I hold tight to, maybe some comment someone made . . . annoyed me . . . (even if it WAS three years ago!). My mind seems to be just chock full of stuff that doesn't need to be there!

Give it up! How do I do that? Turning to Isaiah (again), in chapter 43, vs 18-19:

> *"But the Lord says, 'Do not cling to events of the past or dwell on what happened long ago. Watch for the new thing I am going to do."*

I turn to that verse again as I think about clearing out my mind . . . my memories that tend to weigh upon me. Do you ever have the experience of that little 'spinner' that just keeps spinning and spinning on your computer . . . going nowhere? Until finally you just have to SHUT it down and do a RE-START?

Maybe that's what is happening to us during this time. Maybe we've become so 'full', so 'rich' that we need to just *give it up* . . . clear it out . . . do a 'restart'? It's an interesting concept. Take some time to think about it. I'm working on it.

It does take some patience. Patience with others and patience with ourselves. I'll be sharing the message this weekend . . . talking about patience. Hope you will join us in worship. See you there!

Remember . . . wash your hands, fold them. Bow your head, pray for patience.

Pray with me: "Dear Lord, you know we carry way more than we need. Help us to give up what weighs us down. Give us patience during these days. We pray for all those who are in need, and for caregivers everywhere. Amen. In Jesus' Name, Amen.

We have a statue of St. Francis out on our back patio. There was a similar statue in the same spot when we first looked at our house. It was one of the first items we bought when we moved in. He just needed to be there. Maybe many of you have the same one. He stands there with a bird or two in his hands, occasionally one even lights upon his head.

It's a sign of peacefulness to me. In the quiet morning, I frequently find the words of the prayer of St. Francis coming to me:

> *O Divine Master, grant that I may not so much seek to be consoled as to console;*
> *to be understood as to understand; to be loved as to love;*
> *For it is in giving that we receive, it is in pardoning that we are pardoned,*
> *And it is in dying that we are born to eternal life."*

The words of this prayer are attributed to St. Francis, but it is unlikely that he really wrote them. It doesn't matter to me. What matters is the truth that the words hold.

During these turbulent times I need those words . . . it is so important to be consoling to one another, to be understanding. To give . . . to pardon. For it is in doing these things, that we are born to life forever.

Psalm 29 is often called 'The Voice of the Lord in the Storm". I especially like verses 10-11: "*The Lord rules over the deep waters, he rules as king forever, the Lord gives strength to his people and blesses them with peace."*

Some days peace is hard to come by, much less offer it to one another. But I ask you to think of this prayer when you find your soul troubled, when you are not understood, when you need to be pardoned . . . or you need to pardon. It's hard to understand how peace comes to us, but it does. That is why it is called . . . "the PEACE that **passes all understanding.**" Maybe we don't need to understand it. Maybe we just need to receive it.

May you find that peace this day. Even in the middle of a turbulent storm.

Keep washing your hands. Fold them. Bow your head, Pray for Peace.

Pray with me: "Dear Lord, we come to you in the middle of our storms. We ask you to quiet the waters, give us strength for pardoning and courage to understand. We pray for all in need of healing, those sick in body and those with troubled souls. Bind us together in this peace that passes all understanding. Amen. In Jesus' Name, Amen.

In II Corinthians, chapter 12, vs. 9-10 we read . . . *"My grace is all you need, for my power is strongest when you are weak. I am most happy, then, to be proud of my weaknesses, in order to feel the protection of Christ's power over me. I am content with weaknesses, insults, hardships, persecutions, and difficulties for Christ's sake. For when I am weak, then I am strong."*

As I think about some of my weaknesses, I don't find myself very content or happy with them, how about you? Those verses plague me a bit! I would much rather see myself strong than weak. And it is awfully hard to find much contentment in the present difficulties.

That's what Scripture does for us sometimes. It challenges us to look deeper into our present days and into ourselves. To discover . . . 'when I am weak, then I am strong'.

Remember growing up and never feeling that you were 'good enough'? I did. Most everyone remembers that moment when everyone has been picked for the team and you are left standing! Alone. I wanted to be picked! We all did. But I probably wasn't good enough. I wanted to be the best basketball player . . . but I just wasn't good enough. I wanted to be at the top of my college class . . . but I just wasn't good enough. It took many years, a good deal of scripture reading and the love and support of others to discover that I AM GOOD ENOUGH! And in II Corinthians we are reminded that in our weaknesses – we find our strength.

Ever find yourself calculating your 'net worth'? I have. I add up all the numbers to see what I am REALLY worth. And then I study them and discover that they really don't mean a thing. That's not where my worth is, at all.

My worth lies in the truth that *I am a chosen one* . . . a child of God . . . a member of a royal priesthood. And so . . . I am content with where I am and who I am. I see my weakness and I see my strength. And the best part of all . . . I am GOOD ENOUGH. We all are GOOD ENOUGH! And aren't we fortunate? In this present hardship . . . we are strong.

Remember to keep washing your hands, fold them and bow your heads. Give thanks for this weak moment as we go about discovering our strengths.

Pray with me: "Dear Lord, sometimes we need to be reminded how much you have sacrificed for us. You went all the way to the cross, showing strength in the weakest moment of all. Give us strength for this day and the days that lie ahead. We pray especially for those who suffer, those who are tired of this time and for all who care for others. Amen. In Jesus' Name, Amen.

E-DEVOTION FOR
THURSDAY, MAY 14

I had a roommate in college who used to stand in front of the mirror each morning and say . . . **"I get better looking every day"**. His confidence always amazed me. These days it seems like every morning when I look in the mirror I say to myself . . . **"I look older every day"**!

And that's a good thing, isn't it? In Isaiah 46:4, we read . . . *"I am your God and will take care of you until you are old and your hair is gray."*

I am so happy to hear that Good News! Even as my own body begins to fail me and I see the creases and cracks . . . God is *still* taking care of me. The preceding verse even says..

"I have cared for you from the time you were born." It is so good to know that God has held me in his precious hands from the time of my birth and even now . . . as I get older every day!

It's a reassuring thought, isn't it? No matter what human frailties we experience God does not judge us by our outward appearances. This body . . . this temporary lodging really is just a shell that we inhabit while we journey through this life.

In II Corinthians 4:18 we also read . . . *"For we fix our attention, not on things that are seen, but on things unseen."* As we age we may become a little more content with that thought. There isn't much we can change about our outward appearance anymore. Especially during this time. But we can work on the inside. As we reflect, renew and refresh ourselves 'inside' . . . we may see our 'outsides' a little differently.

So . . . I may not get 'better looking every day', but I do think that during these days I have found my 'inner self' to be a little more grounded. Content? Maybe. I think searching Scripture helps. I hear some of you are reading and studying scripture more than ever. Let's hope it makes us better – in one way or another – every day!

Wash your hands, fold them . . . look at your thumbs in the shape of a cross . . . bow your head, give thanks for one more day of grace.

Pray with me: Dear Lord, we ask for your strength for each and every day. We pray for those who are sick, those who are afraid, those who struggle with the burdens of the moment. We are reminded that you are with us and that you still hold us firmly in your precious hands. Amen. In Jesus' Name, Amen.

MONDAY, MAY 18, 2020

We have two fruit trees in our yard. One is a grapefruit and the other an orange. The grapefruit tree is always loaded with good, large, juicy grapefruit. We don't do much to tend the tree . . . water it, I guess. We really hardly pay any attention to it at all. In contrast, the orange tree gave us 6 oranges last year! We fuss over it, water it, spray it, fertilize and still . . . seriously??? **6 Oranges**?

I can't figure this out. In Matthew 12, vs. 33, Jesus tells us . . . *"To have good fruit you must have a healthy tree; if you have a poor tree, you will have bad fruit. A tree is known by the kind of fruit it bears."*

So what's he telling me? Is the orange tree just 'bad' and the grapefruit tree 'good'? Or is there something missing in the way we treat these two trees? It's a mystery to me.

We know that to bear 'good fruit' we need to be well grounded, rooted, well fed. I was baptized shortly after my birth, started Sunday School at 5 years old, always went to church, youth group, got confirmed. I think I was pretty well fed. Strong in the faith. And yet, there have been times in my own life when doubt, fears, uneasiness has found it's way to me. During those times, my fruit hasn't been that great. So what is Jesus saying to us through this Scripture?

I think maybe that we need to just keep plugging along. Even when our fruit isn't that impressive. When we have doubt. When we are sick and tired of being sick and tired. We search the scripture for encouragement. We pray for diligence. We water ourselves with the Word. We share our difficulties with one another. We just keep on plucking that fruit and one day . . . we are shocked at how juicy and ripe our lives really are!

I'm not giving up on our orange tree. I think there's a lot coming from that thing. I have faith. It's kind of like raising a child . . . some days – good fruit; some days – not so much. But we know that the roots go deep and we just keep on praying for the harvest.

Wash your hands, fold them . . . bow your heads. Bear some good and juicy fruit.

Pray with me: "Dear Lord, give us strength for the day. Soon this time will pass and we will be out and about our daily lives once more. Let us not forget what it took for us to keep watered and fed. This is a time of growing for us, Lord . . . help us to bear good fruit. We pray especially now for our brothers and sisters who are struggling, physically, mentally and spiritually. May our words and our actions be good fruit for those in need. Amen. In Jesus' Name, Amen.

Someone was telling me the story of their neighbor, Maryann. Maryann has been diagnosed with dementia. She always loved her morning walks and so . . . each morning as she heads out, the neighbors keep watch. She frequently becomes confused as to how to find her way 'home'. So, one of the neighbors will step outside and say . . . "Maryann, can I walk you home?" She's smiles gratefully, and off they go . . . sometimes hand in hand.

I heard the expression, not long ago . . . "We are just walking each other home". I really like that. If you have ever sat at the bedside of a dying loved one, it's kind of like that. We are just walking those we love . . . HOME. Sometimes it's just a short walk and sometimes it takes a long, long time.

I could not help but turn to John, chapter 14 when thinking of these things.

"Do not be worried or upset, believe in God and believe also in me. There are many rooms in my Father's house and I go to prepare a place for you." Thomas asks Jesus . . . "Lord, we do not know where you are going, so how can we know the way to get there?"

We all know the answer. Jesus was very clear on that . . . He is the Way, the Truth and the Life. He is the One who leads us home.

Over the years, what we call 'home' has changed many times. A parsonage on the prairie of North Dakota, a house by the lake in Minnesota, an apartment in a city . . . and now, a home in the desert. . .at the foot of the mountains. But it has always been HOME. A place of peace and comfort. Home means many things to many different people. But I really like to think of those words from John . . . a final destination, a home with many rooms. Enough room for even me.

We may have to walk one another home sometimes. It's a pleasant thought, isn't it? To not have to walk alone. To have someone take our hand and lead us to where we are safe. Read John 14. I think you'll find some peace in that.

And don't forget to wash your hands, fold them. Bow your head and give thanks . . . for HOME.

Pray with me: "Dear Lord, thank you for getting home ready for us. For preparing a place for us and for helping us find our way. We give thanks now for those who walk alongside us. We ask for strength especially during these days for the caregivers, the ones who hold our hand as we journey on. Amen. In Jesus' Name, Amen.

FRIDAY, MAY 22, 2020

The other day I was on the phone with someone and he said . . . "Pastor Ken, I just feel so completely HELPLESS." Ever feel that way? That no matter what you do, it just isn't enough. You simply cannot change what is happening.

I was tempted to say . . . "Oh, yes, I know JUST how you feel". But I caught myself in time! No, I don't know JUST how he felt. Not one of us can know how another is feeling, not completely.

So I turned to scripture as I completed that call. Hoping to find some words of encouragement. Because I am feeling kind of helpless, too. I found it! In Hebrews, chapter 4, vs. 15 and 16:

"Our High Priest is not one who cannot feel sympathy for our weaknesses. On the contrary, we have a High Priest who was tempted in every way we are, but did not sin. Let us be brave, then, and approach God's throne, where there is grace. There we will receive mercy and find grace to help us just when we need it."

We may feel helpless, but we do have someone who is there to help us. Ever heard the country western song . . . "I've Got Friends in Low Places"? It's kind of catchy. It's the opposite of "It's not WHAT you know . . . It's WHO you know" I guess it doesn't really matter if you have friends in high places or low places. Not one of them knows exactly what you are feeling when you feel . . . . helpless.

But we do have a friend who 'gets' it. And He is the High Priest. The top one! He knows just what it is to feel so helpless that you almost want to give up. He hung there . . . on the cross, didn't he? But he didn't stay there, or in the empty tomb. He took on the evil of the world . . . and he won! That's a friend in a very high place. **It's someone good to know.**

Remember . . . . keep washing your hands, folding them and bowing your heads. We have a friend who is with us through it all. He feels sympathy for us in our weakness. And He, truly, knows just how we feel.

Pray with me: "Dear Lord, thank you for your gift of grace. For giving us courage to get through the tough times. Inspire us to reach out to those around us who are struggling. And thank you, thank you – for knowing just how we feel. We've got a friend in you. Amen. In Jesus' Name, Amen."

SUNDAY, MAY 24, 2020

I remember one of the first times I ever flew on an airplane and we encountered some serious turbulence. It wasn't just a bump here or there . . . it was serious rock and roll! I was flying alone and trying to be as 'cool' as possible. The young lady next to me said, "Are you ok? Is this bothering you?" As I was attempting to present a 'macho man' image, I replied . . . "Oh, no, I'm fine. This is nothing." Her response . . . . "Well, that surprises me because your white knuckles are blinding me!" **Busted**.

It's hard to fake it when we are going through turbulence, isn't it? The disciples even struggled with that in Luke, chapter 8 . . . it's the story of Jesus calming the storm. Jesus fell asleep and then the winds came up. The disciples panicked and woke him up . . . *"Master! Master! We are about to die!"* Jesus got up and calmed the stormy water . . . then he asked them . . . *"Where is your faith?"*

Some days I just feel as though we are going through a great deal of turbulence. Some of us try to fake it . . . "Oh, no . . . things are fine!" As our knuckles turn whiter and whiter! And some of us ask . . . "Jesus, where are you? Why don't you DO something?"

His reply comes to us clearly. Have FAITH. He has guided us through many storms before and his strong arm is around us through these days as well. One of the things that I love about the church is our heritage of great music. The words of hymns run through my mind many times throughout the day . . . "O God, Our Help in Ages Past" . . . "Faith of our Fathers, Living

Still" . . . "Great is Thy Faithfulness". Our faith is a building block for us when we toss and turn during turbulence.

So when you are feeling a bit 'rocky', things are shaking up around you, picture that scene in your mind. The waves are huge, the wind is roaring, the disciples are scared to death . . . and Jesus is there. He reaches out his arms and the seas are calm, the wind dies down. Just have FAITH.

Wash your hands, fold them, bow your head . . . you don't have to fake it, we're all a little 'shook up' . . . just have FAITH.

Pray with me: "Dear Lord, come to us in our rocky moments. Calm our fears, quiet the storms around us. We hear your voice . . . Have Faith. We pray also for those who suffer in hospitals, at home and for those who are alone. Give us the courage to reach out to our brothers and sisters, to share your calming voice. Amen. We pray all this is Jesus' Name, Amen.

TUESDAY, MAY 26, 2020

Remember when you were a kid and you would pick off the petals on a daisy . . . "Loves me, Loves me not . . . Loves me, Loves me not."? Well, I have to admit I had a 'crush' on a certain little girl in my class and I would do that. It always came up . . . 'LOVES ME NOT'!

Seriously? She really didn't like me very much. I got over the crush as the years went on and even as we became teenagers, I wasn't one of her favorite people.

I've been thinking a lot lately on what it means to 'love one another'. Jesus gives us a clear command in Matthew, chapter 5 . . . beginning with verse 43. *"You have heard it said, 'Love your friends, hate your enemies'. But now I tell you: 'love your enemies and pray for those who persecute you so that you may become the sons of your Father in heaven. For he makes his sun to shine on bad and good people alike, and gives rain to those who do good and to those who do evil."*

I have to be honest. There are times when I just plain don't like someone. I'm human. There are people who do things I just can't understand and it bothers me . . . they are difficult to like. But then these words of Jesus prick at my mind. Can you 'love one another' when you kind of don't 'like one another'? It's puzzling. Especially in these days. People do things that I can't understand. They don't seem to be loving one another . . . or caring for one another . . . or doing what is best for the common good.

But we are to love them, anyway. We should all work on that.

I keep hoping that these times will bring about a kinder, gentler world. That all people will respect the thoughts, words and actions of each other. That we will do the 'right' thing . . . for the common good.

It's puzzling, isn't it? Think about it. And go back to the words of Jesus in Matthew. Lots of teaching there.

And remember to wash your hands, fold them, bow your head. Pray for all people. Those who you love and, especially . . . those who are hard to like.

Pray with me: "Dear Lord, let us hear your word. Help us to understand what it is to truly love one another. To love one another when we don't agree, when we don't understand, when we are finding love a difficult action. Give us strength to care and to do the right thing. Amen. In Jesus' Name, Amen.

THURSDAY, MAY 28, 2020

TRUTH: Sometimes it's a struggle to be truthful, isn't it? Not that we really 'want' to lie . . . but sometimes the truth hurts. So we find ourselves nudging around what we really know we should say . . . but we don't want to say it. Or we say what we certainly should not say.

When our children were young we used to tell them . . . "We may not agree with what you did, or we may not like it . . . but the most important thing is that you tell the truth." And some of the things we would hear were not what we wanted to hear! I remember one time picking my son up from somewhere he should not have been . . . and saying, "What were you doing and what were you thinking?" And his reply still sticks with me . . . . "Dad, you said you would just listen if I would tell the truth."

Jesus was very blunt with the truth. And he was known for that. Mark 12: 13-14:

"Some Pharisees and some members of Herod's party were sent to Jesus to trap him with questions. They came to him and said, 'Teacher, we know that you tell the truth, without worrying about what people think. You pay no attention to a man's status, but teach the truth about God's will for man."

They may have been trying to 'make points' with Jesus, but they spoke the truth. Truth can be a hard thing. But as Christians – right and wrong is very clear to us. We know that when we speak untruths about one another we have done a bad thing. It is our mission to uphold the truth.

These days it's difficult to know what truth is, isn't it? We search for facts and knowledge. We struggle with opinions. Maybe in the end, it's important that we allow the Spirit to speak to us. Jesus told us quite clearly . . . "Do unto others as you would have them do to you". In other words, care for one another.

Remember these words from John 16:13:

"When the Spirit of truth comes, he will guide you into all the truth, for he will not speak on his own authority, but whatever he hears he will speak, and he will declare to you the things that are to come."

Keep washing your hands, fold them and bow your head. Ask God to help you find the truth in all things.

Pray with me: "Dear Lord, there are so many rumblings and messages that we become confused in so many ways. Help us to focus on You and on Your Word. Help us to search for truth in every avenue of our living. For you indeed, are the Way, the Truth and the Life. Amen. In Jesus' Name, Amen.

SATURDAY, MAY 30, 2020

In Luke, chapter 1 we read of the prophecy of Zechariah. It's a scriptural message we usually discover during Advent. It goes like this:

vs. 78-79: "Our God is merciful and tender. He will cause the bright dawn of salvation to rise on us and to shine from heaven on all those who live in the dark shadow of death, to guide our steps into the path of peace."

Years ago we used to take our children to the beach in Florida. We loved picking shells, playing in the surf, making sand castles . . . all the things families do when they make that trip out of the cold Minnesota winter. But the memory that sticks out in my mind the most is when my wife and I would get up early, while the kids were still asleep, and go sit on the beach waiting for the sun to rise. You know . . . that time when dark just seems to creep away and light begins to shine? It's a very special moment. **Watching what God can do.** How He can take darkness away and expose the light.

It's a peaceful moment. It's what I am searching for today. I want that moment when the darkness that surrounds us begins to peal away and the light shines. His promise is that He can do that. *"And to shine from heaven on all those who live in the dark shadow of death . . . guide our steps into the path of peace."*

I'm guessing that's what we all are searching for. Peace. Simple Peace. The good thing is that we believe there is such a thing as peace. May we all search for it . . . may we recognize it . . . may we find it.

And now may the Peace that passes all understanding be yours.

Continue to wash your hands, fold them and bow your head. Pray for peace.

Pray with me: "Dear Lord, we know that you gave us the Prince of Peace. We may be in the moment when darkness seems to be the constant . . . but we also know that your light shines, even in the darkest places. We pray for all who search for peace. Let us be the peacemakers. Amen. In Jesus' Name, Amen.

MONDAY, JUNE 1, 2020

I need to be honest here. I am writing this on Sunday afternoon following a horrendous weekend in our country. I don't know what to say. Period. There are 'no words.'

Have you ever struggled just to pray? I have. Much less to find devotional words to share with you.

The words to the Beatles song . . . "Let It Be" . . . keep running through my head.

> *"When I find myself in times of trouble Mother Mary comes to me, speaking words of wisdom . . . let it be. And in my hour of darkness she is standing right in front of me, speaking words of wisdom . . . let it be. **And when the broken hearted people living in the world agree,** there will be an answer . . . let it be. For **though they may be parted, there is still a chance that they will see.** There will be an answer . . . let it be . . . . .whisper words of wisdom . . . let it be."*

I am praying that the broken hearted people living in the world . . . *will agree.* I am praying that though they may be parted . . . there is still a chance that *they will see.* I am praying for an answer. Let it be . . . Me?

Psalm 46:1-2 says, "God is our shelter and strength. Always ready to help in times of touble. So we will not be afraid, even if the earth is shaken and the mountains fall into ocean depths."

I feel like our world has been hit by an earthquake of great proportions. And we are the ones who are left to live to tell about it. So much anger. So much hatred. So much discord.

And then today, Pentecost. The Spirit comes to move over the land. A new breath . . . the very Breath of God. **This** is the air we must breathe. Sit back, take a deep breath, follow the word of the Lord. Discover that very breath within us. And Let It Be . . . . Me?

I'm not sure it's enough to just wash our hands. Maybe we need to drench our souls. Then bow our heads and pray for one another. Those with whom we agree . . . and especially, those with whom we disagree. Let it be . . . me, who makes a difference.

Pray with me: "Dear God, we are reminded in the middle of all this, that you, truly are in control. That You are our shelter and our strength. That You stand ready to help us in these times of trouble. So we are are not afraid, even though our world is shaken and we feel like we are tumbling into a sea, a tumultous sea. Let us be the ones who speak the truth in love, who share your message of peace to all. Remind us to do what is right, and let it be . . . Me. For You are our refuge and strengh. A very present help. Amen. In Jesus' Name, Amen.

WEDNESDAY, JUNE 3, 2020

I n Mark 12, verse 15 we read: *'Be happy with those who are happy, weep with those who weep."*

I wonder if you have been as close to tears, or perhaps may have shed a few . . . as I have these last days. That verse from Mark just seemed to hit home with me. We know what it is to be happy for one another. Someone has good fortune, their children find success, the worrisome tests come back negative . . . we share their joy! We're ecstatic!!

But when we experience the pain of one another . . . those times can often bring us to tears. Seeing the images unfold on television this past week have done that to me. I am so distraught. And I wonder what words of comfort there are to share?

In the book, *To Kill A Mockingbird,* Atticus Finch says these words to his young daughter: ***"If you can learn a simple trick, you'll get along a lot better with all kinds of folks. You never really understand a person until you consider things from his point of view, until you climb into his skin and walk around in it."***

Those words also made me think of another song from the 70's (or so) . . . **Walk A Mile In My Shoes**. Those words are sometimes attributed to the Native American thought . . . "Walk a mile in my moccasins".

It's true, isn't it? We can't really climb into the skin of another . . . it's also pretty hard to walk for a mile in someone else's shoes. They would probably pinch, hurt . . . even give us a blister or two. But if we **could** do that we may understand a little bit more completely what another soul is experiencing.

We see the images . . . we hear the painful cries. But it is hard for us to truly understand. So we attempt to 'feel' the pain of one another by immersing ourselves in their experiences. Reminds me of the old saying . . . "THERE but for the Grace of God . . . go I."

Empathy is the word. Jesus did it so well. As his followers, those who bear his name . . . let's work on it. Let's try to walk for a few short steps in one another's shoes. It may be just the beginning of a healing journey.

Wash your hands. Fold them, bow your head . . . please join me in praying for some peace to come.

Pray with me: "Dear Lord, we weep with those who weep. We struggle to feel the aches and the pains of others. We pray for empathy. We ask for understanding. But most of all we ask for your healing love to permeate this struggling world. Amen. In Jesus' Name.

Amen.

FRIDAY, JUNE 5, 2020

For those of you who grew up in the northern plains, I am sure that you remember those good old snowstorms! We lived on a farm in central North Dakota and I remember full well having to 'do the chores' no matter how the wind blew and the snow flew! There was one particular snowstorm that was so fierce but the trek from the house to the barn still had to be made. There were cows to milk!

That late afternoon my father took out a long piece of rope and tied it around my waist. I wasn't sure what was going to happen next! Then he held onto the other end of the rope . . . told me to step into his footprints in the snow as we made our way to do the jobs that needed to be done.

That memory came into my mind today as I heard the words of the song, *"Bind us together, Lord . . . Bind us together. With cords that cannot be broken. Bind us together, Lord, bind us together. Bind us together in love."*

I also found myself reflecting on the words of Ephesians 4:3 . . . *"Do your best to preserve the unity which the Spirit gives by means of the peace that binds you together."* Not finding a lot of peace these days, are we? But there is hope in all things. I was able to watch parts of the memorial service for George Floyd in Minneapolis today. There were so many poignant images. People standing together for over 8 minutes to acknowledge the last moments of this man's life. And then, as the cars left the scene . . . Minneapolis police and fire fighters on the curb . . . taking a knee.

There is hope. There are people who are full of faith that

we CAN and WILL be bound together. There are good people . . . and yes, there are bad people. Nothing new about that. But there is also that strong rope . . . that cord . . . that binds us together. That binds us together in LOVE.

Continue to wash your hands, fold them and bow your heads. We will come through these days because we are people of faith . . . with HOPE.

Pray with me: "Dear Lord, grant peace and harmony and healing to our land. Give us strength for the walk. Let us look for the footprints to follow. Keep us bound together. Unify us in your name above all names . . . Amen. In Jesus' Name, Amen.

SUNDAY, JUNE 7, 2020

As I was wondering what message to share with you today we received a text from our daughter-in-law. They were out in the boat on Leech Lake in Minnesota and she sent a photo of this deer swimming towards shore. Now, Leech is a big lake that covers 111,527 acres. So picture in your mind this little deer just swimming like crazy. We wondered . . . can it make it? A short time later her text came through . . . "It was an amazing swimmer . . . we watched until it made it to shore! All good."

Persistence. Keeping your 'eye' on the goal. Staying focused. All those words come to mind. And then, also the words of Philippians, chapter 3, verse 14:

> "So I run straight toward the goal in order to win the prize, which is God's call through Christ Jesus to the life above."

Sometimes it is very difficult for us to keep our eyes on the goal, isn't it? Life throws us one curve after another. Family worries, financial concerns, illness, the world seems to be in a complete mess. But then this passage of Scripture reminds us to stay focused. To find the 'center' of ourselves.

I thought about that when I saw that photo of that beautiful creature just swimming along. Such power! Such strength! Such determination! What a lesson for us today. Just keep swimming, little deer! And for you and I, also . . . turn to the cross, run straight ahead with strength. There are these hurdles that can trip us up. There are curves and uphill climbs and crashing waves. But we know where He is directing us to go. We have a goal. We have a purpose. And at the end of that chapter in Philippians, we read . . .

"Put into practice what you learned and received from me, both from my words and from my actions. And the God who gives us peace will be with you."

I remind you folks, keep washing your hands, fold them and bow your heads. Give thanks and focus on what is right and true. **And just keep swimming!**

Pray with me: "Dear Lord, you are our constant. You are our strength. You are the One who unites us and gives us the power to keep going. We pray now for those who struggle, those who feel overwhelmed and afraid, those who may be losing the determination to keep going. Let us be the ones who bind up the brokenhearted, help heal the hurts and point others in your direction. Amen. In Jesus' Name, Amen.

JUNE 9, 2020

Grace . . . a gift to be celebrated! At Desert Hills we hear that a lot . . . It is the first phrase in our mission statement. In fact, we have those words above our patio door on our back patio. "Celebrate Grace"! That reminds us every day that Grace is something to be celebrated!

In Ephesians, chapter 2, verses 8-9 we read these words:

"For it is by God's grace that you have been saved by faith. It is not the result of your own efforts, but God's gift, so that no one can boast about it."

My mind went to 'gifts' today as we celebrated a birthday in our house this week. What gift can I possibly give to show my love . . . my appreciation? No gift is big enough. Nothing seemed . . . 'right'. And then those words from Ephesians came into mind. It is the greatest of all gifts. The gift of grace/love. There is nothing I can do. Nothing at all to make me or someone else worthy of such a gift. It's not by my own doing. It's just there . . . the gift of grace. Free.

We give gifts to one another. Sometimes it's because we feel we 'have' to. Sometimes it's because we want to show appreciaton. Sometimes we just do it out of duty. But the most beautiful gift we have to give to one another is that reflection of God's grace. The gift of love. It may not be something tangible. It may be just a word . . . or a gesture . . . a block of time . . . a smile. It may the best gift the other person receives on any given day.

And receiving a gift? That's a beautiful thing, as well. Sometimes we just have to open our hearts to receiving something we don't feel we have any right to receive. So think today . . . about the gifts you can give and the gifts you receive.

Amidst all the turmoil, frustration and unrest in this world . . . take some time . . . to "Celebrate Grace"! Take the time to give something of yourself to someone. It may be the best gift they will receive. God's **Grace** . . . **G**od's **R**iches **A**t **C**hrist's **E**xpense . . . open your heart to receive . . . open your heart to give.

And . . . wash your hands, fold them . . . look at those thumbs in the shape of that cross . . . bow your head . . . give thanks for the Grace that is ours in Christ Jesus.

Pray with me: "Heavenly Father, we thank you for the gift of your Son, Jesus Christ. You have poured the riches of your grace upon us. Open our minds and our hearts to share your love and your grace with those we encounter on our walk these days. Amen. In Jesus' Name, Amen.

JUNE 11, 2020

For some reason I seem to have an 'internal' alarm clock that wakes me up around 3 a.m . . . *Every* morning. I know that I'll fall back asleep but I usually get up, turn on the TV in the other room and watch the weather channel. There's something about growing up in the midwest that makes you a 'weather watcher'!

The other morning I watched as the television showed a major storm with high winds, rain and tornadoes was moving right through the middle of the country. My first thought was kind of selfish . . . "Thank goodness we aren't driving up north through that right now!" We've done it many times. Going across Kansas or Nebraska with our eyes peeled on the skies wondering if those big, black clouds were heading right for the highway.

Those thoughts brought me to the words from Matthew 7:24-25 . . . *"Every one then who hears these words of mine and does them will be like a wise man who built his house upon the rock; and the rain fell, and the floods came, and the winds blew and beat upon that house, but it did not fall, because it had been founded on the rock."*

Now we know that Jesus is not talking about our physical homes. He is reminding us of the strong foundation upon which our faith is built. That doesn't mean that 'because I am a Christian' no matter what comes in life, I will be spared. Oh no! We're still going to face our storms . . . but it is in **how** we deal with those storms that matters. It is **how** we speak and act from that firm foundation that people discover how active our faith is. From Emerson, we get this quote . . . *"I cannot hear what you* *say, for what you are **thunders** in my ears."* And there is a lot of thunder out there . . . in our world.

Keep your house in tact. Even when the storms are raging. I have heard it said: "Of the early Christians it was observed, 'See how they love one another, and they are turning the world upside down.'"

Our firm faith is active in our love. That is a great challenge when the storms come.

"Our hope is built on nothing less than Jesus' love and righteousness . . . On Christ, the solid rock I stand. All other ground is sinking sand."

Remember to keep washing your hands, fold them, bow your heads. Give thanks and keep the faith.

Pray with me: Dear Lord, Keep us upright, rooted, firm in our faith. And give us strength to speak words of love and mercy. We pray for all people as You have taught us to do. Amen. In Jesus' Name, Amen.

SATURDAY, JUNE 13, 2020

I've been thinking a lot about Jesus as the Good Shepherd lately. Some days I feel like a 'lost sheep' and I am in need of someone to give me some good pointers on what direction I should go. Ever have times like that?

In Matthew 9:36, we read: *"As he saw the crowds, his heart was filled with pity for them, because they were worried and helpless, like sheep without a shepherd."*

I like that picture that comes into my mind . . . THE COMPASSIONATE JESUS. We read about him over and over again in scripture. "He had compassion on them . . . " He sees right through us when we struggle or need his direction.

Growing up on a farm I learned early what to do if we saw a sheep who had either become wet with rain, or had stumbled and fallen. The sheep would roll on it's back. No matter how it would kick and squirm, it just couldn't 'right' itself. So we would have to take the feet and gently roll the sheep upright. It may wiggle and wobble for a bit, but eventually it would be able to walk and join the rest of the flock.

That experience is in my mind as I write this today. Sometimes I feel as though I have 'tipped' over. I'm flailing in the 'wrong' direction! And then the COMPASSIONATE JESUS is there for me. He reaches down and sets me upright once more.

Compassion . . . study the word. It's nothing more than what we are taught about in the Beatitudes, The Sermon on the Mount, The Ten Commandments . . . Confirmation, and through the words, "Do onto others as you would have them do to you".

I'm feeling a little more 'upright' today! How about you? We have the Good Shepherd to lead us through these many valleys and on up to the mountaintop! Thanks be to God, for HOPE.

Keep washing your hands, fold them each time you do . . . bow your head. Give thanks.

Pray with me: "Dear Lord, you have shown us the way to compassion. Strengthen us in our daily living so that we do what we know is right. We pray for healing for those who are ill, comfort for those who mourn, direction for when we feel a little bit 'upside down'. Amen. In Jesus' Name, Amen.

Psalm 118:24 . . . "This is the day the Lord has made . . . let us rejoice and be glad in it."

I usually write this devotion the day before you receive it. So I am writing this early on Sunday morning. We just 'went' to church . . . online, of course. We sat outside with our laptop, on our back patio. The birds were in full chorus. A butterfly or two flew by, the sky was that incredible shade of blue that we see so often here in Arizona. Our main distraction was a bee that seemed to want to disrupt our worship.

Those words from Psalm 118 just kept running through my head. **This is THE DAY!** I have this entire day ahead of me. And even though I know full well that there is a terrible fire raging near by, that the news of the day may be upsetting, that the Coronavirus is still very concerning, I am going to live THIS DAY to it's fullest!

I hope that doesn't appear uncaring or selfish. My heart is still full of love and concern for our brothers and sisters who are unable to live this day as I can. But I know that God has given us each just this ONE day to feel the fullness of his love. This one day is the day that we are given to find ways to share that fullness of love.

So I sit back and take in the beauty that surrounds us. I rejoice that the Lord has given us this day. I plan to live it to the fullest. And when it comes to day's end . . . I will give thanks that He has allowed me to have this one day. When and IF I wake tomorrow . . . . guess what? I will have that ONE MORE DAY to rejoice and be glad in it!

So let's rejoice together! Let's make everything count on the ONE DAY that we are given. Let's work toward healing and safety for all people. Let's be THE CHURCH . . . and most of all, let us make our discipleship alive in love and action.

This is the day the Lord has made! I am SO glad for that! Wash your hands, fold them. Bow your heads and give thanks for THIS DAY.

Pray with me: "Dear Lord, thank you for today. And for my to-morrows. Our prayers go out for those whose days are difficult, who struggle to find the sun, who crave for the soft breezes of the day. Make us instruments of your peace to give hope to the hopeless, love to the loveless, courage to the faint and peace to all who suffer. Amen. In Jesus' Name, Amen.

During this time of 'staying at home' we've been watching a lot of movies. Some are excellent. Some just plain stink. When we watch a movie that is not particularly good . . . we'll look at each other when it's over and say . . . "Well, that was just a complete waste of our time."

I'm imagining that many of you have had a similar experience.

We watched a movie the other night that was about a man whose child was kidnapped and he was asked to pay a large ransom. He didn't hesitate for a moment. His immediate response was . . . "No price is too high! I will pay anything to get my child back!"

Those words have played in my mind. No price is too high . . . I will pay anything to get my child BACK. In Matthew 20: 28, Jesus says . . . *"Just as the Son of Man did not come to be served, but to be serve and to give his life as a ransom for many."*

What was God thinking? He **gave** His Son. No price was too high. This wasn't a deal done in a back room somewhere . . . here's the money . . . now you get your Son back. No, this was a brutal struggle. A test between good and bad. A battle played out on a hill. And for what? For folks such as you and I?

It's just so unbelievable. But I believe it. Because the Father's love is that great. You could watch that in a movie and say . . . "Great scene! He gave up his only son. Played very well." But this is real life. This is when the Father sent his Son to us . . . to you and to me. Paid the ransom. Every day I just marvel at that fact.

So go with this thought . . . God so loved this world, this messy, complicated world . . . and EVERYONE in it . . . that He gave us His only Son. As the body of believers, THIS is the message we can carry into that world . . . To serve and love one another. 'Not to be served . . . but to serve.' Find a way to serve . . . show compassion . . . exhibit grace . . . let this be what they say about us . . . *"See how they LOVE one another"*. No price . . . too high.

And wash your hands, fold them . . . bow your head. Give thanks for the Greatest Story Ever Told.

Pray with me: "Dear Lord, we thank you for the gift of your Son. Forgive us our shortcomings, our pettiness, our distrust of one another. Grant us courage to show your love in all the ways we can. Amen. In Jesus' Name, Amen.

FRIDAY, JUNE 19, 2020

I was spending some time the other day reading through Proverbs. There's a wealth of information and direction in that book! As I read, I came across Proverbs 18:24 . . .

"Some friendships do not last, but some friends are more loyal than a brother."

I'm lucky as I have a brother who over the years has become a close friend. We're far apart in age so it took us awhile to learn some things about one another. In any case, we're good friends now and I am grateful for that.

I also starting thinking about a very good friend of mine who just had a heart attack and has been recovering. I'm thankful that he is better. I have another friend who is facing some challenging tests, possible surgery, etc. at the Mayo Clinic in Rochester. I'm worried about him and pray for him every day.

Sounds like my friendship circle is aging a bit, doesn't it? That happens to us at this this time in life. I love the kids' song . . . "You've got a Friend In Me" . . . . I'm sure you've heard it. There isn't anything I can do to make a friend's life simpler or better . . . but the knowledge that they 'have a friend in me' goes a long way.

You know where this is going! Yes . . . What a Friend we have in Jesus! When our road is rocky, the going gets tough it is so good to know that above all else . . . He is our Friend. We never walk these dusty, difficult roads alone. There are so many people who have passed through our life . . . some have 'moved' on . . . and some have remained for the long haul. I don't think I have expressed my appreciation for friendship often enough . . . I'm working on that.

But one thing to me is crystal clear as I reflect on these words from Proverbs . . . loyal friendship is a precious commodity. As we have all been a little isolated lately we may have found ourselves working a bit harder to connect with our friends. When we feel very alone it is good to reach out to others.

And when you feel apart from our best friend, Jesus . . . just know how simple it is to reach out for him. He's right there, I promise you. He will never desert you, leave you alone or forget you. It's a good thing to KNOW you have a friend.

I speak with so many of you on the phone and I can sense how lonely some of you are. But you are not alone. Do not forget that.

And remember . . . wash your hands, fold them and bow your heads. Be thankful that we not only have a friend in our Lord, Jesus Christ . . . you've got friends in many places. Give a special thanks for our church family.

Pray with me: "Dear Lord, thank you being a friend. Our true and faithful friend. Help us to remember that you are always with us, that you are our best friend. Amen. In Jesus' name, Amen.

SUNDAY, JUNE 21, 2020

In Luke 4:10 we read:

"He will command his angels concerning you, to guard you carefully."

We leave for Minnesota for our long awaited visit with our children and our grandchildren this week. Needless to say . . . we are so excited! Especially after this long time of 'sheltering in'.

This will be a happy time for all of us as we have felt such a sense of 'distance' during these days.

I refer to that verse in Luke because we are a little wary of travel during these times. It is a period of discontent in so many avenues. It is a time when we must place our trust in God's angels to carry us safely to our destination.

On one of the first flights I ever took the music playing over the airplane audio was John Denver's *"Leaving on a Jet Plane"*. I remember it so well . . . that feeling of lifting into the sky, the music, and the sensation of TRUST that I had. It was as if the very hand of God was lifting me from one safe place to another. That's what our God does, isn't it? When we place our trust in God we find ourselves carried . . . . sometimes from a place that creates confusion, stress, anxiety . . . on to a place of refuge, solace and peace.

I am praying that will happen for all of us. That as we struggle through uncomfortable days we find that the only thing to do, is to TRUST. Trust that God is very much in control and He will see us through.

Envision me sitting on my son's dock . . . grandkids right there . . . sharing the moments with one another . . . the lake is still . . . loons are calling. Peace beyond measure.

Remember to keep washing your hands, fold them, see your thumbs in the shape of that cross. Give thanks . . . give thanks for one another.

Pray with me: "Dear Lord, we trust that you will guide us from one place to another. That you will lift us in your powerful hands and carry us through stormy days. We pray for peace with all people. We ask that, as your servant folks in this world, we may be the peacemakers. And now . . .

"MAY THE PEACE THAT PASSES ALL UNDERSTANDING BE YOURS IN CHRIST JESUS."

Amen. In Jesus' Name, Amen.

TUESDAY, JULY 21

In Psalm 150, verse 6 we read: *"Let everything that has* **BREATH** *praise the Lord!"*

WOW! I feel as though I have been filled with a brand new breath. That's what 'time away' or 'vacation' as some of us refer to it . . . does for you. It's always good to come home, but being in Minnesota this past month with our family seemed to give me new breath . . . wind 'beneath the sails', so to speak.

The night of July 4th we were fortunate enough to be out on Leech Lake in Walker, MN on a boat with our son and family. It was an amazing night. We started to take pictures of the sunset and it just kept getting better and better. Finally, we *just quit*! We all sat back and enjoyed the moment. Then a large, beautiful sailboat floated by and it felt like the breeze just gave it that little 'lift' . . . it was a breath of air that filled my lungs and lifted my spirits. The full moon was an added spectacle and that last burst of fireworks had us cheering and clapping with enthusiasm. It was wonderful to see how much our grandchildren enjoyed those moments. Almost as much as we did!

I have heard it said that Psalm 150 is like the **GRAND FI-NALE** to the Psalms! Just like that burst of color and light that filled that northern Minnesota sky. Those words, *"Let everything that has breath praise the Lord"* popped into my mind that moment. I couldn't help but feel that my spirit had been filled with 'new' breath.

Ever have those times when you feel as though you just can't take another breath? I have. We have all struggled with the isolation and uneasiness we still feel during this pandemic. On top of it all, we have faced difficult and troubling days as a nation. What is it that we need? How about a burst of new air? Start reading the Psalms over again . . . and when you get to Psalm 150 . . . imagine it as a GRAND FINALE! **Let these words fill you with a breath of fresh air!**

Monsoons are 'acomin' . . . I hope we can all enjoy some refreshing rain . . . and a breath of new, fresh air!

In any case . . . we need to keep washing our hands, folding them, bowing our heads and giving thanks for the air we breathe..breath is a wonderful thing.

It's good to be home! Talk soon!

WEDNESDAY, JULY 22, 2020

Whenever I fly, I always want the window seat. There is just something about watching the earth fade away as we rise up into the clouds.

I was thinking about this verse from II Corinthians 4:18 when we left Minnesota on the first part of our journey back to Arizona:

> *"So we fix our eyes not on what is seen, but on what is unseen. For what is seen is temporary, but what is unseen is eternal."*

As we lifted off I could see many familiar landmarks . . . the Mall of America, the lakes, the Foshay tower. It was a scene I knew well. Then we passed through some clouds and I couldn't see a thing. It was as if I had lost perspective. All of a sudden, the clouds moved away and there was that bright blue sky! It was an 'aha' moment.

Often we are comfortable in the familiar. Life goes on, day after day, and nothing shakes us. Then we go through some 'unfamiliar' times. Like moving through those clouds, in a way. It's hard to keep perspective. We aren't sure if we are headed in the right direction. On a plane . . . we just trust the crew and the navigation system. But in life there are times we aren't sure who or what to trust. We may lose our perspective. Hopefully, we get through those days and the clouds fade away and we can see clearly once again.

Whenever we have gone through some hard days as a family, I liked to remind our children to try to 'view' the situation from 30,000 feet up. I found myself doing that as our plane lifted us higher and higher. *"What is unseen . . . is eternal."*

Well, my feet are back on the ground again. Thanks be to God, for that. I'm sure I'll lose perspective again and again. But from 30,000+ feet up . . . I have been reminded that it is vital to 'fix our eyes' on what is unseen. For that is eternal.

As we keep washing our hands, folding them (remember those thumbs in the sign of the cross) and bowing our heads . . . keep perspective. And continue to pray for one another, our church, our community, our nation and our world.

And . . . trust the Pilot. Amen.

FRIDAY, JULY 24, 2020

Have you ever struggled to forgive someone? I'm guessing you have. Most of us have had that fight. We KNOW we are supposed to forgive but sometimes it's just so hard.

Colossians 3:13 says . . . *"Be tolerant with one another and forgive one another whenever any of you has a complaint against someone else. You must forgive one another just as the Lord has forgiven you."*

Be tolerant? Sometimes that's tough. And then the verse also says.."You **MUST** forgive one another. How direct is that? There's no gray area there. Intolerance is just

NOT tolerated! So, in other words . . . if someone does or says something to me that I find so offensive, I still need to forgive them? And tolerate them, too?

That's pretty direct in line with the life of Christ. He tolerated all kinds of people. People who were not tolerated by others. People who did nasty, horrible things. Even directly to Him. Like spitting at him, whipping him, even hanging him on a cross. His reply? "Father, forgive them . . . for they don't know what they are doing."

So my struggle with forgiveness when I have been wronged, may be similar to yours. We MUST forgive. The Bible tells us that very clearly. Remember when the children were small and they would go on and on and on about something someone had done to them? Finally we would say . . . FORGIVE THEM! And GET OVER IT!

The funny thing about when you forgive someone it seems

as though some heavy load you have been carrying around is gone. It just drops away. No use dragging that old resentment around anymore. And as we move on, we may even find that we can forgive ourselves for our intolerance and our resentments. That's the best part. Walking lighter without that inner anger and that bitterness.

Wash your hands, fold them, bow your head and ask for forgiveness. And when we do that, we can go ahead and forgive that old 'wrong' that has been 'bugging' us for far too long. It's easier than we think . . . and something we MUST do. Lighter baggage, easier to carry!

Pray with me: "Dear Lord, give me the strength to forgive. And help me forgive myself, too. Inspire within us all a new tolerance . . . a new understanding. Give strength to all who feel unforgiven, those who are ill and those who are caregivers. In Jesus' Name, Amen.

Amen.

TUESDAY, JULY 28, 2020

In Mark 6, verse 31 and 32 we read: *"There were so many people coming and going that Jesus and his disciples didn't even have time to eat. So he said to them..'Let us go off by ourselves to some place where we will be alone and you can rest a while' So they started out in a boat by themselves to a lonely place."*

When we hear the words, 'lonely place', we may think of it in a negative way. Being 'alone' and being 'lonely' are really two different things. Sometimes a lonely place is a good thing. Ever find the need in a group of people to just take your mind away . . . to a lonely place? Where you can set aside all the chatter and just be 'alone' with your thoughts?

Our youngest granddaughter has a very cool swing that hangs from a large willow tree in their backyard. A swing that has been in that spot since she was very small. They need to adjust it frequently as she grows. I noticed many times this past month during our visit, that we would all be in the yard, laughing, talking, eating . . . and Ella would just get on her swing and swing away. Sometimes she would even put on her earphones. I asked her one day . . . "What are you listening to?" Her response was . . . "Sometimes music but sometimes nothing." She is a very wise 10 year old!

In middle of all the fun, she seemed to need to get away. Into her own 'lonely place'. I saw that as a good thing. I find myself having that need more and more these days. And I think of Jesus . . . and his disciples . . . the clamor of the day must have been stifling for them. He had the good sense to take them away to a 'lonely place'.

When you find yourselves unable to listen to the 'din' much longer, just follow his lead. Take yourself away to a lonely place. Take a few moments to reflex, relax, and maybe pray. It's a clamoring world out there. But in our own quiet moments of calm, there is a good place. Maybe a lonely place . . . a quiet place. Where we are met by his peaceful presence and maybe we are inspired to bring that peace of God into the tumult of our world. Through our own peaceful reflection God comes to us and strengthens us for our work . . . our ministry . . . our mission.

Pray with me: "Dear Lord, we are finding ourselves in crazy, difficult places some days. Help us to find a peaceful presence. A peace that passes all our understanding. A peace that inspires and directs us to step out of our place and bring comfort and calm to those around us. Calm the storm. Quiet the winds. Give us peace. Amen. In Jesus' Name, Amen.

THURSDAY, JULY 30, 2020

Ever felt like you will NEVER get from 'Point A' to 'Point B'? In other words, times are tough and you think you may not get through this present situation?

The people of Israel kind of felt that way . . . and then they were reminded of the word of the Lord. In Joshua 1:9, we read: *"Remember that I have commanded you to be determined and confident! Do not be afraid or discouraged, for I, the Lord your God, am with you wherever you go."*

I heard just this week about a young woman, a medical professional in an emergency room in Colorado. She has contracted the Coronavirus. She has a family, brothers and sisters, parents, husband, children. She was just out there doing her job. I'm sure she did everything right and was extremely cautious. But now her family faces a very present danger. My heart aches for them and I wonder what words will give courage.

I struggled with those thoughts and then the words from Joshua came to me. "***Do not be afraid or discouraged, for I, the Lord your God, am with you.***"

Isn't is something to discover that no matter where we walk or whatever comes to us, we are never alone? Getting from 'Point A' to 'Point B' might be a long difficult struggle but as we pass **THROUGH**, (and remember it is something we go **THROUGH**) the hard times, God is right there beside and within us. We all need a bit of encouragement these days. I heard someone say the other day, "I will never be so happy to see a year go by then 2020!" I agree. It's been hard on many people. There are young families who worry about sending their children to school, some cannot come up with a mortgage payment, some see the possibility of their job, their lifetime work, being taken away. Then . . . there is this young woman in Colorado. Most likely sick . . . and scared.

As we face tomorrow let's all take a moment to sit back and pray for one another. Pray for encouragement for each other. Pray for healing. Pray for strength for the day. Pray for better times. And pray for everyone to discover that each person is not alone. God has reminded us in Joshua, very clearly . . . *"Do not be afraid or discouraged, for I, the Lord, your God, am with you."*

And remember to wash your hands, fold them, bow your head and give thanks. For He is there . . . right beside you.

Pray with me: "Dear Lord, sometimes we feel so all alone. We feel like the waters are washing over us and we simply struggle to breathe. Help us to find comfort and strength in your words that You are with us, every step of the way. And grant healing to all who are sick, give strength to those who care for others, give comfort to those who are afraid of what lies ahead, give us empathy to identify with those who struggle through life. Amen. In Jesus' Name, Amen.

TUESDAY, AUGUST 4, 2020

Whenever I share in the words of the Confession of Faith, I always find myself 'pinched' a bit when I repeat . . . "And the things I have left UNDONE".

As I may have mentioned before . . . I am a list maker. Every morning I make my "To Do" list. When we first moved to Green Valley and I was actually 'retired', our neighbor stopped by one morning. My 'to do' list was laying on the counter and Joel said.."What's this?" "My 'to do' list", I replied. His response . . . "Don't you get it? You don't have to do anything!"

But I often do leave things undone . . . or unsaid. I am reminded of the words of Isaiah, 42:16: "*I will lead my blind people by roads they have never traveled. I will turn their darkness into light and make rough country smooth before them. These are my promises, and I will keep them without fail.*" Some translations say . . . "*I will not leave them undone.*"

I am always disappointed with myself when I leave things undone. Sometimes we do the things we should not do and we don't do the things we should. So I confess . . . I am sorry for the things I have left undone.

God is leading us (sometimes we *are* blind) down some roads we have never traveled before. He promises to turn our dark days into lighter days and our rough road will be smooth once again. That's His Promise. He doesn't leave His promises undone.

So what to do? I see so much anguish, frustration, sadness, anger, sickness in our world and I feel as though there is little

I can do to change things. I confess . . . I'm leaving a lot UN-DONE. But I am not working through this alone. His rod and his staff comfort me. He leads me. And He gives me the words that I try to keep before me. There isn't much I – one person – can do. Or is there? Our main job, our primary focus is clear: "Love the Lord, your God with all your heart, mind and strength. And love your neighbor as you love yourself." Each one we meet is in great need of that love. And it is through this love, I really believe this . . . . that I can get some things done. Maybe not all on my 'to do' list. But the world is in great need of that message. Love your neighbor. Just the way you love yourself.

No room for undone there.

And remember to keep washing your hands, fold them, bow your head and ask God for the strength to get things done.

Pray with me: "Dear Lord, we know that through your kept promises we have the ability to get things done. We ask for your guidance as we walk the stony path. We ask for your presence when we feel like leaving things 'undone' or 'unsaid'. You are our constant companion. Thanks be to God for that. Amen, In Jesus' Name, Amen.

THURSDAY, AUGUST 6, 2020

One of the favorite passages in the Bible is in John 14: . . . *"Do not be worried and upset,"* Jesus told them. *"Believe in God and believe also in me. There are many rooms in my Father's house, and I am going to prepare a place for you. I would not tell you this if it were not so. And after I go and prepare a place for you, I will come back and TAKE YOU TO MYSELF, so that YOU WILL BE WHERE I AM."*

Some translations say . . . . *"I will take you INTO MY PRESENCE."* I love that thought . . . 'into my presence'.

Have you ever been in the presence of someone who just brings a sense of comfort or calm? We are fortunate when we discover people in our lives who can do that for us.

In my very first parish we had a neighbor next door. She was a widow now living alone in her small house. I would go over there at times when I felt especially stressed or frustrated with my work. There was just something about entering her house, sitting at her kitchen table with a cup of coffee that brought me back to center. Alphie had that 'presence' about her. It almost seemed as though she would 'take me into herself'. We didn't have to say much. It was her PRESENCE that brought me peace.

Sometimes I find the presence of God in unlikely places. In nature, of course. Many of us have experienced that. In worship, and often when I find myself just sitting in the church sanctuary all alone. And sometimes I find God's presence in the middle of people. It's a strange thing. Hard to identify. And then many times I find the presence of God when I am all alone with just my thoughts.

I find it so calming to know that there is a place ahead for me . . . a house with many rooms and God has prepared a spot . . . just for me. He wouldn't tell me that if it were not so. So God has gone ahead and will take me into that presence . . . some day. My old friend Alphie was a theologian in her own right. She didn't need to speak many words to strengthen this young, struggling pastor. She just would welcome me into her presence. Good Lord, I pray that in some small way I can share that presence with someone, as well. Don't you?

Wash your hands, fold them . . . and keep praying. The very presence of God is around and within you.

Pray with me: "Dear Lord, we are so grateful to be in your presence. Help us to recognize those moments when we find ourselves just a little bit lost. Inspire us to walk with others into your presence, as well. Amen. In Jesus' Name, Amen.

TUESDAY, AUGUST 11, 2020

Who is my neighbor? In Luke 10, we read the Parable of the Good Samaritan. The teacher of the law asks Jesus . . . *"What must I do to inherit eternal life?"* *Jesus gives a quick response . . . "What does the Scripture tell you?"* *And the man goes on . . . "Love the Lord your God with all your heart, soul, strength and mind. And love your neighbor as you love yourself."* *Jesus tells him he is absolutely right. Then come those words . . . "Who is my neighbor?"*

Then . . . that loved parable of the Good Samaritan. We all know the story very well. But who, really, is my neighbor? I have a number of folks in my neighborhood. I don't know all of them very well . . . but I like the ones I know. Maybe I even 'love' them. They're pretty much like us. Retired. Keep their yards nice. Wave when they go by. They're actually quite easy to love. Some of them I may not agree with on certain points . . . but that's okay. I like them. I guess I love them.

So I'm home clear. Right? Eternal life! HERE I COME!

And then the words of that great hymn nudge at the back of my mind . . . *"I, the Lord of sea and sky, I have heard my people cry. All who dwell in dark and sin, my hand will save. I who made the stars of night, I will make their darkness bright. Who will bear the light to them? Who shall I send? . . . . And I hear: HERE I AM, LORD. IS IT I, LORD? I HAVE HEARD YOU CRYING IN THE NIGHT. I WILL GO LORD . . . IF YOU LEAD ME. I WILL HOLD YOUR PEOPLE IN MY HEART."*

I have heard it said that the nature of God is to show mercy. Not hate. Not distrust. Not fear. Not anger. Mercy. How do I love my neighbor? And WHO is my neighbor? God just keeps nudging me with those words . . . **"Who shall I send?"** And I really want to respond . . . **"Here I am . . . Send ME!"** My neighbor is the nurse working the ER. My neighbor is the mailman who delivers my mail. My neighbor is the cop getting a coffee at Starbuck's. My neighbor is the child who is afraid of the dark. My neighbor is the refugee who has no where to lay his head. My neighbor is the young bride blown off her feet by the explosion in Beirut. My neighbor is the homeless man in the wheelchair in Reid Park in Tucson.

I could go on and on. But today I just need to remember that God's love and mercy will only be shown through me when I recognize who is my neighbor. And I hear the words . . . "Who will I send? And I know the answer very well . . . "Send me. I will go, Lord . . . If you lead (need) me. I will hold your people in my heart." **ALL YOUR PEOPLE**.

Remember to keep washing your hands, fold them, bow your head. Hear the words of the Lord . . . "You go, then . . . and do the same."

Pray with me: "Dear Lord, break our hearts of stone. Give us hearts for love alone. It is our calling to be better. We CAN be better. We CAN DO better. Unite us these days to see our neighbor. And to be a better neighbor. Amen. In Jesus' Name. Amen.

THURSDAY, AUGUST 13, 2020

Hebrews 13:2 . . . *"Be not forgetful to entertain strangers; for thereby some have entertained angels unaware."*

Many, many years ago Dale Evans Rogers, the wife of Roy Rogers, wrote a little book entitled "Angel Unaware". It is the story of their small daughter, Robin, who lived only a short time. We've had it in our personal library for years and I came across it just the other day. As I sat down and read it I found myself thinking of the many 'angels' I may have encountered over these years . . . many 'unaware'. Angels who have touched my life in large ways and some whose brief encounter made an impact I didn't realize at the time.

Dale Evans Rogers, in her foreword to the story, says . . . "It has been said that tragedy and sorrow never leave us where they find us." I have also found that to be so very true.

A number of years ago a young family in my former parish found themselves in a similar place as their newborn son was born with serious health issues. They spent time at the Mayo Clinic in Rochester, MN as doctors worked endlessly to make this baby comfortable in his distress. He died after a short time and the moment we spent at his graveside is indelible in my mind. This family was changed forever. Through this sadness they have learned to experience joy in a very new way. They will celebrate the marriage of their oldest daughter this fall and I know through all their celebration and happiness the memory of that little boy, that angel, will still be fresh and uppermost in their minds. Tragedy and sorrow have taken them to a new place.

Look around you for those angels of whom you may not be aware. As I mentioned just the other day . . . they are your neighbors. Some are harboring an old sadness . . . a tragedy. Some are struggling with a sorrow long hidden. It is our mission, as the people of God, to lift one another out of a dark place on to a new and level place.

Jesus tells the story of the banquet feast . . . some chose not to attend. So what did the host send his people out to do? To go to the highways and the byways and invite in the 'stragglers', the 'struggling', the 'hungry', the 'lonely'. We can do this. It is our job. It is our calling. It is our mission.

Please keep washing your hands, fold them and bow your head. Ask God for help in making the world a better place.

Pray with me: "Dear Lord, open our eyes so we can see. Open our ears so we can hear. Open our hearts so we can love. Continue to make us aware of the angels around us. Those who strengthen us and those who need our strength. Fill us with your love and give us your peace. Amen. In Jesus' Name, Amen.

TUESDAY, AUGUST 18, 2020

In Psalm 51:10, we read: *"Create a clean heart in me, O God. And renew a right spirit within me."*

I love sharing those words with the congregation in worship. And every time I say them, I think to myself . . . "O God! I need a CLEAN heart! And I sure do need a RENEWED SPIRIT!"

A number of years ago a gentleman in a former parish received a heart transplant. The heart he received was from a young boy killed in a car accident. It was such a time for mixed emotion. One family filled with joy at a chance for new life. Another family broken hearted with sadness. I remember so well his words . . . "How lucky am I? I get a brand new, clean heart! An old guy like me!"

And he did. He began his life again with a new heart. Wouldn't it be wonderful to do that? To take our old heart, full of some anger, some fear, some frustration and start over with a brand new clean one?

Sometimes I feel as though my heart just aches. It aches for those I care about who are struggling. It aches for the church as we try hard to make a difference in the world. It aches for our world. It just seems that we are getting so much wrong. And then those words from Psalm 51 come to me . . . *"Create in me a clean heart, O God"*. God can do that. He can take what it is that bears down upon us and God can lift those worries and fears from us. God has the power to give us a clean heart. To renew a right spirit within us.

That's the Good News I want to share today. That God's Spirit is alive and working in our world. Working through people like you and me. Working through the church. Reminding us that loving and caring for our neighbor, whoever that may be, is a part of a 'heart cleansing'. As we open our hearts and our lives to one another God's Spirit permeates through us. We need to find a way to help one another have a 'heart cleansing'. There just is no room in our hearts for mistrust, anger, fear . . . all those things that give us a heavy heart.

So today . . . take a deep breath before you wash your hands, take a deep breath before you fold them and bow your head. Take a deep breath and ask God to create within us, all of us, a new heart. A heart that is open to the Spirit . . . a heart that will be renewed.

Pray with me: "Create within me a clean heart, O God. And renew your spirit within me. Give me patience, give me kindness, give me peace. And may your Holy Spirit wash over us and give us all peace. Amen. In Jesus' Name, Amen.

THURSDAY, AUGUST 20, 2020

We've all heard the saying . . . "Beauty is in the eye of the beholder". I had a conversation recently that reminded me of that old adage.

I was telling someone about our trip north and mentioned that we had especially enjoyed our drive across my birthplace, North Dakota. The fellow looked at me questioningly . . . "Really? I've only driven across that state once and I thought it was boring. No trees! Just flat land!"

I feel kind of badly that I didn't go into my tirade about the beauty of that flat land but I decided to just let the subject drop.

For beauty truly is . . . just in the eye of the beholder. What I see . . . you may not see. What you see . . . I may see totally differently. When we looked upon the horizon on that day we saw the amazing golden color of grain, we saw the beauty of that 'big sky'. We marveled at how green the fields were. Someone else might just drive across Interstate 94 and see nothing but highway for miles and miles.

As I've thought about that conversation I wonder if what I see may be colored by my experiences. In my mind I see myself driving a tractor across that field, in my mind I see my grandfather, a Norwegian immigrant, picking peonies to take to neighbors. In my mind I see that white wooden church with full pews, people singing their hearts out . . . "For the Beauty of the Earth".

God challenges us through scripture to open our eyes that we may see. Some of us have unhappy past experiences that color what we see. Some have good memories that allow us to see very clearly.

Reflect on these words from Psalm 119: *"Open my eyes . . . that I may see"* . . . and try to see things just a little differently. Perhaps from someone else's point of view. So often we go around with our eyes closed – our hearts set. Yes, beauty may just be in the eye of the beholder. But I can't help but believe that there is great beauty to be found . . . just by opening our eyes. Even on the straight and open road.

Remember to wash your hands, bow your head, give thanks for the beauty not only of God's amazing creation . . . but the beauty we can see in one another.

Pray with me: "Dear Lord, give me eyes that I may see. Give me ears that I may hear. Give me a heart open to love. And help me find beauty – goodness – kindness – empathy and understanding all around me. Amen. In Jesus' Name, Amen.

TUESDAY, AUGUST 25, 2020

I enjoy listening to good music. We have a CD player outside so often in the early morning I will drop a favorite CD in the player and let my mind wander as I reflect on what I listen to. The other morning I thought to myself . . . "Wow, these guys really know how to harmonize". The blending of the different voices over their varied ranges was so pleasant.

What is harmony? I guess it's simply put as simultaneous music notes that blend together for a pleasant effect. Not everyone sang the same note. That would have been pleasing, maybe, but would not have the same impact as the blending of different sounds made by different people.

In Ephesians 4, Paul writes about the unity of the body. *"Do your best to preserve the unity which the Spirit gives by means of the peace that binds you together."* I urge you to take the time to read all of Ephesians 4. It gives us an interesting blueprint for our life in Christ. And it ends with those powerful words . . . *"Instead, be kind and tender-hearted to one another, and forgive one another, as God has forgiven you through Christ."*

Basically . . . live in harmony. What a wonderful message for these days. Harmony doesn't mean we all have to stay on the same note. That might even be monotony. No, we don't have to agree or think exactly the same. But Paul urges us in this scripture to work diligently to preserve the peace that will bind us together. To show respect to one another. To honor one another. To build one another up, not tear each other down.

It's basic Christianity, folks. Ephesians 4 lays it out for us very clearly. It's about feeling the pain of one another . . . not causing the pain. It's about speaking kindly . . . choosing our words carefully. I remember Mr. Larvick, our high school choir director, who so carefully corrected our 'off' notes. I remember him saying, "That's not QUITE "harmonious"! I think he was kindly telling me that I wasn't destined for a great musical career! But in his correction, he still made me feel as though I was an important part of our Boy's Quartet. It's about building up the body in the spirit of love and harmony.

So let us use these challenging days to think about living in harmony. No, we're not all on the same note (or maybe even the same page) but we still respect each other and we strive for the bond of peace we share.

Keep on washing your hands, please bow your head and offer prayer for those who struggle, those who continue to care for the sick and the dying, those who make decisions for us, those who lead and those who follow.

Pray with me: "Dear Lord, give us the power to weigh our words carefully, to think before we speak, to show love and compassion and to be the ones who bring harmony to our home, our church, our community, our nation and our world. Amen. In Jesus' Name, Amen.

THURSDAY, AUGUST 27, 2020

Have you ever been driving down a secluded road at night and your headlights go out? I have. Believe me . . . it's a scary situation! It happened to me on a lonely road in a snowstorm once and I will never forget the sense of fear that came over me. All of a sudden the darkness just seems to envelop everything and you can't see your way at all.

I was reading the Beatitudes again the other day and for some reason I kept on reading in Matthew, chapter 5. The scripture goes on to speak of salt and light. The passage from vs 14-16 really hit home with me . . . *"You are like light for the whole world. A city built on a hill cannot be hid. No one lights a lamp and puts in under a bowl; instead he puts it on the lampstand, where it gives light for everyone in the house. In the same way your light must shine before people, so that they will see the good things you do and praise your Father in heaven."*

I see way too much darkness right now. And when I think about that passage from Matthew I remember our children singing that little song . . . **"This little light of mine, I'm gonna let it shine! Hide it under a bushel . . . NO! I'm gonna let it shine!"** And I cannot forget how LOUDLY they would shout **NO**! I feel as though it's time to shout **NO**. All the division, anger, frustration and fear that we sense around us needs a word . . . and that word is **NO**. As the people of God, we are much better than this. When we see something or hear something that builds distrust or unhappiness or despair for others, it's time to say **NO**.

Let your light SHINE! I'm not spewing any certain view, etc. But I do know, as a follower of Christ that I need to shine a light on a dark place. If each one of us took out that light and let it shine maybe we'd be in a better spot. It isn't just 'doing good works' so that others will see what we do and give praise to God . . . although that's a good thing! It's a change of attitude . . . seeing the best in all people . . . it's showing respect for humankind and it's shedding a light in some very dark places.

Washing your hands is still vitally important . . . we need to stay safe and well. Then we need to bow our heads, fold our hands and ask God for direction. For Him to lead us and give us courage to turn on the lights, reject the darkness and show love . . . not hate. We live in a beautiful world, folks . . . let's turn the light of God's presence on . . . all around us.

Pray with me: "Dear Lord, we ask for guidance. We ask for strength. We ask for healing. Give power to your people to be the light. Lead us. Amen. In Jesus' Name, Amen.

THURSDAY, SEPTEMBER 3, 2020

When I was little and my mother would ask me to do something I didn't care to do, I remember her words . . . "Just do it for 'my sake', Kenneth". For a very long time I didn't understand what she meant. I remember thinking . . . "I don't want to do it for 'her sake'. I don't want to do it at all!"

That's an interesting thought, isn't it? Doing something not for our own purposes but for the sake of others. The word 'unselfish' comes to mind. My little jobs to do weren't really that difficult. I'm sure she could have accomplished whatever it was she wanted in no time at all by doing them herself. Especially in light of the time it took for her to listen to my immature whining and complaining! Parents, can you identify?

I guess she was trying to teach me a lesson. Her plan was to help me learn that what I do, I don't always need to do for the pleasure or the satisfaction of myself. But some things we do, some stands we take . . . are for the good of others. The good of all.

Jesus reminds us of this thought in Matthew 10:9 . . . *"Whoever tries to gain his whole life will lose it; but whoever loses his life for my sake will gain it."*

I had a good mom. She worked hard on the farm and was not the type to shirk from duty or responsibility. When I look back over these 70 some years I wish I would have done more 'for her sake'. But her lessons did not just come to me about farmwork or helping around the house. She taught me a few lessons on doing for others, on working toward a greater good for all. The needs of the extended community were important back in those days on the farm. Taking vegetables to neighbors, raising a barn when it was necessary, plowing the field for a neighbor who broke his leg.

It didn't matter what positions anyone held, or what opinions they had. I am sure there were many arguments, down right battles between neighbors back then as well as now. But it just seems like we could look past much of that as we worked together for the common good.

Like Jesus says . . . *"Whoever loses his life **for my sake** . . . will gain it."* Take some time to think about how to act and what we say that actually builds up the community . . . the church . . . our country and our world. Let's all start thinking about what we say and do that is actually, **for the common good**. Words are one thing . . . actions speak much louder.

I'm lucky I had a mom who asked me to do those few little tasks . . . "for her sake".

Keep on washing your hands, we're not in the clear yet! Then fold them, bow your head and pray for the building up of all people . . . for the common good.

Pray with me: Dear Lord, give us insight and wisdom to do what needs to be done. Amen. In Jesus' Name, Amen.

TUESDAY, SEPTEMBER 8, 2020

I've been doing some Old Testament reading and I stumbled into Jeremiah. Now that was a guy with a lot of stress! He seemed to be very frustrated with the people of his day and in chapter 7, verse 16, the Lord even tells him . . . *"Jeremiah, do not pray for these people. Do not cry or pray on their behalf; do not plead with me, for I will not listen to you."*

Wow. That's not the message we hear very often from God. Kind of hard to grasp, isn't it? Back in chapter 6, verse 16, we read . . . *"The Lord said to his people . . . 'Stand at the crossroads and look. Ask for the ancient paths and where the best road is. Walk in it, and you will live in peace."*

It seems as though the people of Israel were at a crossroad. Ever been there? I have. There is a decision to be made as to which way to go. We look one way . . . looks promising. Then we look the other way . . . that looks good too. What to do?

It's a crossroad. Either way may be the right way. We just don't know for sure. There are no guarantees. I remember back when one of our children was struggling with a major decision. **"Dad! Just tell me what to do!"** Well, good old dad didn't have the answer either. I do remember saying, tho' . . . *"Think it through very, very carefully and *you will walk into the answer.* It's right there in Jeremiah . . . *"Walk in it and you will live in peace."*

As we all struggle with decisions these days, for most of us, our ultimate goal is PEACE. We just aren't always sure which road will take us there. That's why I really love to look into scripture. Those ancient words have so much truth for today. We find ourselves struggling with opinions, attitudes, options and ultimately, decisions. Thinking carefully and clearly we hear the words of Jeremiah . . . *"Ask for the ancient paths and where the best road is. **Walk in it and you will live in peace.**"*

At a crossroad? Think, pray . . . and soon you will 'walk into the answer'. I guarantee it.

Please keep washing your hands, fold them and reflect on that cross your two thumbs makes . . . bow your head and ask God to help you make good decisions.

Pray with me: "Dear Lord, so many times in life we find ourselves taking the wrong turn. Help us to think through our decisions, to ask for your guidance and then go beside us as we 'walk into the answer'. Amen. In Jesus' Name, Amen.

THURSDAY, SEPTEMBER 10, 2020

"REMEMBER ME" . . . . these words that Jesus spoke are so important. We remember Him through the bread and the wine, through words of scripture and in our daily thoughts. Remembrance is a very special gift.

I love Philippians 1:3 . . . *"I thank my God for you every time I think of you; and every time I pray for you all, I pray with joy because of the way in which you have helped me in the work of the gospel from the very first day until now."*

Every time I read those words I find myself thinking back to my very first parish in North Dakota. I remember my first day . . . I remember my first worship service and I remember the very first time I shared the Holy Communion with those good folks. And that was about 50 years ago!

Now . . . don't get me wrong. I admit I probably can't remember what I had for dinner three days ago . . . I forget where I put my keys . . . (haven't found them in the refrigerator yet, thank goodness!) . . . I have moments when I go into the kitchen and have no idea what I was going to do. We call those 'Green Valley Moments", don't we?

But there are some moments in life which are just so impressive that we don't forget them. I remember the day the men from the parish drove up to our apartment at Luther Seminary in a grain truck to move us to our first home. I remember how excited we were to see our 'treasures' loaded in that truck and how happy we were to get on the road. Years later they laughingly told me that they thought about just stopping off at a dump and unloading and then taking us to the nearest furniture store! They were such good and generous folks and I thank God many times for learning about how to be a pastor from them.

Jesus says . . . "Remember Me". He has become such a real part of our lives that how could we ever forget Him? But sometimes we do. We lose our way, we struggle to believe, we doubt . . . and we are afraid. And then our minds are flooded with a host of memories . . . ways He has carried us and strengthened us and been our 'rock' in the past. And those are the times when the taste of the bread and the scent of the wine come back to us and we know he is In Us . . . he is With Us . . . he is Our Body, Our Blood.

Remember . . . to wash your hands. Fold them, bow your head, say a prayer. Give thanks for all those wonderful memories . . . never forget who you are. And WHOSE you are.

Pray with me: Dear Lord, we remember how generous you are to us. So generous that you gave us your only Son . . . your only Child. The One who is with us as we travel through this life. We thank you for that great gift. Strengthen us in our journey as we reach out to one another, sharing your strength and showing your love. Amen. In Jesus' Name, Amen.

TUESDAY, SEPTEMBER 15, 2020

Isaiah 43:1 . . . *"Israel, the Lord who created you says, 'Do not be afraid – I will save you. **I have called you by name – you are mine.**"*

I remember when our kids were little and they would come home, off and on, with the cry . . . "He/She called me A NAME!" We would ask, "What did they call you?" Sometimes it was just plain funny but sometimes the name was hurtful.

What's in a name? When we had our children it was a major decision to choose a name. Because that name would identify this person for all of his/her life. It's a big deal to carry a name. I love my name 'Nyhusmoen'. It is Norwegian and it means 'New House in the Meadow". I remember going to Norway and standing at the grave of my great grandfather and seeing that name while looking out upon a beautiful green meadow. That moment rang so true to me as to what that name meant and what those generations of Nyhusmoens' had gone through for me to carry that name.

Our daughter is adopted. When she married some years ago she told us that she would be keeping the name, Nyhusmoen. Her husband was very comfortable with that decision and we asked her 'why?' Her reply . . . "My name is one of the most wonderful gifts you gave to me."

I don't like name calling. Never have. Never tolerated it in our children. What we call one another is extremely important. It is the Lord God who called us by name. He gave us His Very Own Son's Name. That's a big deal. Our daughter and our sons are proud of their name, I can tell that. Just as proud as we are. It's not a 'haughty' proud. It's a love of what came before us and what we can pass on to children and grandchildren.

We are called by Jesus' name. We are called Christian because we are a part of His great family. A family that has been handed a strong, loving, caring name. And Isaiah goes on to remind us in verse 1 . . . *"When you pass through deep waters, I will be with you. Your troubles will not overwhelm you. When you pass through fire, you will not be burned; the hard trials that come will not hurt you. For I am the Lord, your God, the holy God of Israel, who saves you."*

So wear your name proudly. Stand up for the name of Christ. For no matter what comes our way God is with us through fire and fury. Through the good days and the hard trials. His promises are real and true.

Please keep on being careful, washing your hands, fold them, bow your head and thank God for giving you His Name.

Pray with me: "Dear Lord, there are fires burning, hard trials and difficult days. We are so grateful that you go with us down these roads. Thank for calling us by name . . . with your name. Give us strength to carry on and give us empathy and caring to be aware of the needs of others. Amen. In Jesus' Name, Amen.

THURSDAY, SEPTEMBER 17, 2020

Last fall we took a trip to Spain. We had a great guide who directed us on some very interesting paths. We traveled the northern part of the country and on our journey we encountered various pilgrims who were going The Way . . . the path to Camino de Santiago. It's a sacred walk, some trails are easy . . . flat land, open road, clear direction ahead. And some of the paths went down rocky inclines, through all kinds of vegetation, etc. Along the Way we would see the markings . . . the small shell shape . . . showing the path ahead.

We met some pilgrims who were only going a short bit. And some who had made the commitment to go the entire Way. Interesting people with various reasons for taking this journey.

I have thought so much about that trip lately. Wondering what happened to some of those folks. One man, in particular, was going on the journey in honor of his wife who had died just months before. "It was always something we planned to do together", he said. "Now I am doing it alone – but not really. She is with me."

Our life roads are like that, aren't they? We plan, we plot, we contemplate how the trip will go. Some trips we take with family and friends and some journeys we just need to do on our own. Sometimes we think we have it all figured out. Then we have some stumbles, some things block our way, we falter. But yet . . . . we press on.

Read Philippians 3 . . . *"the one thing I do, however, is to forget*

what is behind me and do my best to reach what is ahead. So I run
straight toward the goal in order to win the prize, which is God's call
through Christ Jesus to the life above."

We return to a soft opening of worship this weekend. Due to my own health concerns and after discussion with my family and my doctor, I feel it is best for me to not worship in the sanctuary with you at this time. However, I will certainly be worshiping 'full force' with you via online and will be, along with all the hosts of heaven, rejoicing at the Good News that we are One Family in Jesus Christ, our Lord.

Keep on being safe, washing your hands, folding them and bowing your head in prayer. As we ALL *press on* to the goal that is before us through the promises made to us by God, our Father and our Brother and Keeper . . . Jesus Christ.

Pray with me: 'Dear Lord, we give you thanks that you are very much with us as we travel down these various paths. We ask for healing and strength to travel the rocky way. We are so grateful we do not walk alone. Amen. In Jesus's Name, Amen.

TUESDAY, SEPTEMBER 22, 2020

In Colossians 2:7, we read . . . *"Keep your roots deep in him, build your lives on him, and become stronger in your faith, as you were taught. And be filled with thanksgiving."*

Having lived in Northern Minnesota for many years we always love to take a fall drive to see the leaves turn color. Our granddaughter sent us a picture this last weekend of the beautiful trees on the road to their home. It makes us a bit homesick for the beautiful fall 'up north'. But then . . . we know very well what comes next! Brrrrrr . . . .

When we purchased our home here in Green Valley one of the selling points for us was a large pine tree on the golf course right in our backyard. It's a huge tree. So many mornings while we are having our coffee we speak of how much that 'touch of Minnesota' comforts us.

That tree is so big that it must have a great root system. The saying goes . . . "The larger the tree, the more rooted it is". To grow strong, roots are very important. I also love the saying from J.R.R. Tolkien . . . *"Deep roots are not reached by the frost"*. In other words, if our roots are deep the difficulties that come our way may be a little bit better to bear.

Being rooted in Christ . . . growing stronger each and every day is an essential part of our living as Christians. Even at this age, there is so much room for growth, isn't there? But just having good roots isn't everything. We need to keep ourselves fed and watered. Scripture, prayer, study . . . those are good ways to feed our souls. And then, we think about what we produce! The fruits of the spirit, of course. In our world today *we are the ones* who can spread our branches and produce good fruit. This is a time for us to show love, mercy, compassion, empathy, kindness, sensitivity . . . all those things that one who has strong roots can spread.

Think about how deep your roots really are. Just from a little seedling, watered in our baptism, fed through years of Sunday School, Bible School. Nourished by teachers and pastors, parents and family, friends and neighbors. And now a grown tree . . . kind of like that pine tree in our backyard. It gives us afternoon shade, it reminds us of where we came from, it gives home to birds who build their nests. And it continues to lift branches to the sky.

"Rooted in faith" . . . we grow and share our lives, our stories and our faith.

Keep washing your hands, fold your hands, bow your head. We're not out of the 'woods' yet! And give thanks for roots, deep and strong that carry us through all time.

Pray with me: "Dear Lord, we thank you for the gift of faith. The gift born in us and nourished with love. Give us strength to share the fruits of your love with all people. Keep us strong, protect us and help us be the shade to those who need our healing presence. Amen. In Jesus's Name, Amen.

THURSDAY, SEPTEMBER 24, 2020

Most of us are familiar with this beautiful verse from Isaiah 40: *"But those who trust in the Lord for help will find their strength renewed. They will rise up on wings like eagles, they will run and not get weary; they will walk and not grow weak."*

When we lived on the lake in Minnesota we would watch the bald eagles fly above us. Seeing them swoop down and grab a large fish in their talons and then soar above our house was so exciting! I remember talking with an 'old timer' once about the eagle. My old friend told me that the eagle, as compared to other birds, would not fly to a place of hiding when a bad storm was near. No, the eagle would fly towards the direction of the approaching storm, flying directly into the wind and using the current of the storm would lift it's wings to fly higher . . . flying above the storm. I'm not sure if that's true or not, but I like to think it is.

I never hear verse 31 from Isaiah 40 without thinking of that story. The eagle trusts that the winds of the storm will not overcome it . . . but will just make it stronger and give it the ability to rise above the storm.

A lesson for us today, isn't it? I walk . . . and I get weary. I can't imagine 'running' any day soon! But the Lord reminds us in this passage that it is our TRUST in Him that renews our strength. It's just a matter of **trust**. Trusting that the winds of the present storm will not overtake us. Trusting that we have the strength to RISE ABOVE and have our strength renewed.

So whatever the storm is . . . and there are a few raging, aren't there? **TRUST**. Trust in the strength that comes from the Grace of God to carry you above the fierce winds. *"You will rise on wings like eagles . . . you will run and not get weary . . . you will walk and not grow weak."*

That's the promise He gives us today . . . and every day.

Wash your hands, fold them in prayer, bow your head and be renewed, not weary, never faint.

Pray with me: "Dear Lord, You were there for us in the beginning and you will be with us in the end. You carry us each and every day. We ask for your continued guidance and your strong arms to keep us in your care. Amen. In Jesus's Name, Amen.

TUESDAY, SEPTEMBER 29, 2020

When we meet one another, perhaps in the parking lot of the grocery store, or at a place of business, I have been accustomed to greeting people with a smile. It's just the way I grew up. So these days, while we wear our masks . . . I find myself smiling as I walk into the Safeway . . . at first it bothered me that no one seemed to be smiling back. And then I discovered that if I looked the other person right in the eye . . . I could easily tell that I was receiving a smile in return, even though their face was partially hidden.

Maybe you have had a similar experience. For a time it appeared as though we had eliminated smiling at one another. The mask seemed to become something to hide behind.

The quote, "The eyes are the window to the soul" is attributed to Shakespeare but we find many references in scripture to that thought. In Matthew, chapter 6 we read . . . *"The eyes are like a lamp for the body."* Interesting thought, isn't it? Our eyesight is very precious. We realize that more and more as we get older. And then again . . . in some ways, maybe we begin to see things a little more clearly.

Our thoughts, our vision can become so clouded these days. I remember hearing the story of a little girl who had terrible vision. Her parents had no idea how difficult it was for her to see until a perceptive teacher mentioned that she didn't participate in class when lessons were written on the blackboard although she seemed to be quite sharp. She suggested they have her eyes tested. Of course! Her vision was very impaired. The morning she received her new glasses she was so excited when she walked outside and saw the leaf shapes on the trees! A whole new world opened up for this child. (And by the way, that child was my wife!)

Maybe we all need to take a new and fresh look around us. Maybe our lives have been a bit too cloudy lately and we have found our vision . . . our perspective . . . a little impaired. Just a thought.

Keep on washing your hands, fold them in prayer, bow your head and ask God for clearer vision. And by the way . . . look into the eyes of that next 'masked' person . . . share a smile! You may be amazed at what you will see in return.

Pray with me: "Dear Lord, give us clarity. Guide us and direct us in all our ways. Forgive us for the wrongs we have done to others. Strengthen those who work so hard among us . . . doctors, nurses, technicians, police, delivery folks, teachers and students. Help us to share through our eyes, what it is that is in our soul. Amen. In Jesus's Name, Amen.

THURSDAY, OCTOBER 1, 2020

We had an exciting afternoon last Sunday. We were able to watch via 'live stream', our 11 year old granddaughter, Ella, at a swim meet in Hopkins, MN.

I don't really understand all the technicalities of 'live streaming' but it sure was a miracle to me that I could sit at my kitchen counter in Arizona and see her little, but very powerful, body push through that 100 yard free style swim to pop up out of the water in first place! She called me when she got to her phone and I said, "How did you do it? How did it feel?" Her reply . . . "I could tell no one was beside me and I knew someone was close behind but I just kept going and pushed ahead!" Both of us were so proud of not just her skill . . . but her PERSEVERANCE.

That's what it takes! Perseverance! We know that from Romans 5 . . . *"We also boast of our trouble, because we know that trouble produces endurance, endurance brings God's approval, and His approval creates hope."*

We press on. This present life has many difficult times. Many people are struggling with physical difficulties, especially in our community and our church. Some have had death touch their lives and now find life as they knew it changed forever. Sometimes we are not as strong as we wish ourselves to be. Romans goes on in chapter 5 . . . *"For when we were still helpless, Christ died . . . God has shown us how much he loves us . . . He has made us his friends through the death of his Son."*

Those words are just so powerful. When we are at our weakest, we look from one way to the other . . . we push ourselves forward for we know that what it is that is behind us will not overtake us. Take some time to read and study Romans. God's promises are there for us. But for this day . . . we will PERSE-VERE! We press on for the prize that is ours in Christ Jesus, our Lord.

Wash your hands, please. Be very careful. Take time to fold your hands and look at the cross formed by your thumbs . . . bow your head. Give thanks for the power that is within us to move forward . . . to press on . . . to persevere.

Pray with me: "Today, dear heavenly Father, we ask for your guidance. We pray for the power to move ourselves forward. To not concentrate on what is behind us, but to look ahead. To look to the cross as we move forward. Give us strength to lift those who falter, give us kindness to share your love and give us peace. Dear Lord, we pray for peace. Amen. In Jesus' name, Amen.

TUESDAY, OCTOBER 6, 2020

Do you remember your mom or your dad saying these words . . . "You need an ATTITUDE ADJUSTMENT, young man!" I sure do. And I think it's an admonition we used on our own children many times.

Sometimes how we respond to what life hands us is just that . . . all about attitude. Paul, in his letter to the Romans puts it this way . . . *"Do not conform yourselves to the standards of this world, but let God transform you inwardly by a complete change of your mind. Then you will be able to know the will of God . . . what is good and is pleasing to him and is perfect."*

Paul is telling us in this letter to not be tempted to follow what the world would 'think' our response to life *should* be but to have a complete change of mind.

When life hands us unbelievable challenges it's hard to direct our attitude in a certain way, isn't it? Our little flower girl at our wedding many years ago, is a mother of three, a wife, a hard worker in her profession. We have always loved her deeply and have always thought of her as such a positive person. She faced the breast cancer that took over her body this past year with her typical 'go get 'em girl' ATTITUDE. Oh, I'm sure she has had her moments and her fears. She's no 'Pollyanna', that's for sure. But as we visited with her just the other evening I realized it was her ATTITUDE that was bracing her for this battle. There are many in our own congregation that are going through similar moments. Finding the right 'attitude' to get through these days is no simple task.

That 'attitude adjustment' does not come easily. That's for sure. As we cheer one another on from the sidelines we strengthen each other by Paul's words of transformation. We find courage from one another as we brace each other up during the hard times. Some days the 'right' attitude is very difficult to discover. The world seems to lead us in one direction but through this scripture Paul is reminding us that we can, through the power of our loving God, discover a complete change of mind as we move forward.

So hang in there folks! Maybe an 'attitude adjustment' is necessary many, many times throughout each day and throughout each struggle we face. But God empowers us, carries us and strengthens us as we walk together down each and every path.

Please wash your hands, fold them, bow your head. Pray for strength, not just for yourself, but for one another.

Pray with me: "Dear Lord, we pray for those who suffer, those who face difficult days and those who have struggles beyond our comprehension. Let us be the ones who lift up, who give strength, who walk beside. Amen. In Jesus' Name, Amen.

OCTOBER 8, 2020

I am looking forward to being able to share the message with you this coming weekend. As I thought about the text I had chosen . . . it's the story of the banquet feast where many people turn down the invitation, I started to think about the word, HOSPITALITY.

Hospitality is actually an 'industry'. It's a business. Who would have thought? Just by acting 'hospitable' you can actually turn it into a money making venture! Through the years we have enjoyed our travel experiences . . . going out to new and different restaurants, staying in resorts with our family or finding unique and different hotels to have a 'get away'.

Lately . . . not so much. We hesitate going out to eat and we certainly don't do any traveling right now. It's a bit disappointing. Even our friends with whom we have enjoyed sharing meals are not so comfortable doing that. So have we lost our sense of 'hospitality'?

I don't think so. There are many references in Scripture about being hospitable to one another. We all know about welcoming strangers, don't we? But I think in these days we can take hospitality to a different level. We may not be able to invite one another to a meal (the banquet) because we are being cautious, but we can find ways to be hospitable. In Romans 12, we read . . . *"Be happy with those who are happy, weep with those who weep. Have the same concern for everyone . . . . . .do everything possible on your part to live in peace with everybody."*

Good advice for days when we aren't feeling very hospitable, don't you think? As we share in the worship this weekend, be it online or in place, reflect on what it means to receive the invitation to that great banquet. Think about finding your place, but not only a place for you, a place for others. Although we may not be able to share in meals physically with one another we can find some simple ways to feel a part of each others lives. To weep with one another through the difficult days and to be happy, to laugh with one another when there is some joy to share.

As we shared some weeks ago . . . being hospitable may even mean 'entertaining angels unaware'. Our world is in grave need of kindness and understanding . . . that's what being hospitable is all about. I shudder when I hear so much discourse and I wonder what I can do to change the climate of just plain nastiness. And then I read Romans and I get a little clarity. It's a simple fact. Loving one another as we love ourselves, that's really what it's all about.

So please keep on washing those hands, folding them in prayer. Bow your head and ask God to open your heart for more room for 'hospitality'.

Pray with me: "Dear God, direct us in all our ways. Help us to search out ways to welcome strangers, to love more deeply and share the peace that is ours in Christ Jesus. Amen. In Jesus's Name, Amen.

OCTOBER 13, 2020

I was visiting with my cousin by phone recently and we were reminiscing about the 'good old days'. We talked about how we could just hop on bikes and go wherever we wanted. We were as 'free as the birds'! And not only that . . . we were strong and fit and mighty!

It was shortly after that conversation that I was reading John. Oh my. I came across chapter 21, verse 18. "*I am telling you the truth; when you were young, you used to get ready and go anywhere you wanted to; but when you are old, you will stretch out your hands and someone will tie you up and take you where you don't want to go.*"

Well, here we are. Acceptance. Jesus is telling his friends that they may have to go somewhere they don't want to go. And he is headed to the cross.

My cousin's husband has been ill and has had to go to a nursing home. So after 60+ years of marriage they find themselves . . . each of them . . . in places they didn't want to go. I get that. And I struggle for the words to help her get through these times.

Sometimes acceptance is a very difficult thing. When you were young did you ever open up your arms and spin around and around until you just fell to the ground laughing? I remember the freedom of that experience. Now I find myself closing my arms, sometimes even wrapping them around myself and letting the strength and the power of God engulf me. That can be a very freeing experience, as well.

Are there words of courage here from Jesus in John? I think

so. We learned so much as children, as we grew and life changed for each of us. We learned that there are so many things we simply cannot change. For one reason or another, life hands us some challenging times. Maybe we can't spin around and let go like we used to, but we can find ourselves in the loving arms of our dear Father. And we accept what it is we cannot change.

I love the hymn, "Breathe on me, Breath of God . . . . fill me with life anew". It may be a different life then we had planned but we relax in his loving arms as he holds us close.

Remember to wash your hands, fold them and bow your head. Give thanks for this loving God who is the same today as He was yesterday and will be tomorrow.

Pray with me: "Heavenly Father, there is so much in life that we struggle to accept. We really would rather have it 'our way'. Help us to place all our cares and our struggles in your wide open hands. We give thanks for your breath that fills us each and every day new. Thank you, thank you. Amen. In Jesus' Name, Amen.

OCTOBER 15, 2020

Have you ever done something that you just cannot forgive yourself for? I'll admit it. I have. I've been forgiven by the person I wronged but it still just keeps lurking there in the back of my mind. How do we get rid of that thought?

When we share in confession we often say: "If we say we have no sin, we deceive ourselves and the truth is not in us. But if we confess our sins, he will forgive us and free us."

OK. I get it. But that 'wrong' still sits there. I guess what it is, is that we need to forgive ourselves. That's a struggle. It almost seems as though we want to hang on to that ache and keep on blaming ourselves.

Give it up! Take the words of Jesus to heart. YOU ARE FORGIVEN. And believe it! When we have given up an old hurt it's just amazing how much better we feel, isn't it?

Back in the Bible Camp days we would have a campfire and the young people would sit down and write any old hurt, anger, resentment, 'sin' on a piece of paper. As the fire burned, they would toss those papers in the fire and sit back and relax. I'm sure many of you shared in a similar experience. As adults, maybe we need a good old bonfire to toss some of our old hurts away.

I visit so many times with folks who just can't seem to 'get over' what hurt they have caused or what hurt has been done to them. So when we speak those words of confession, let's take them to heart. Let's forgive one another for what has been done. But even so much more important . . . it's time to for-

give ourselves. "If we confess our sins . . . He will forgive us."
They say that confession is good for the soul. It's a cleansing,
of sorts.

It's time to give it up. Let it go. Confession said. Forgiveness
given.

So when you wash your hands the next time, fold them and
bow your head. Thank God for forgiveness . . . for one another
and for ourselves.

Pray with me: "Dear Lord, too often we hang on to old hurts
that just seem to take a spot in our soul. Help us to give them
over to you. And thank you, for being the loving, forgiving God
that you are. Amen. In Jesus' Name, Amen.

TUESDAY, OCTOBER 20, 2020

Do you ever find your heart just filled with thankfulness? Back in the 'old days' when I was a young intern pastor we had a pastor in the church I served who ended every single prayer with . . . "we are thankful and grateful". At the time, those of us on staff would find ourselves snickering a bit. "Why does he always double talk that? Can't he just say 'thankful' without 'grateful'?"

As I got to know him better through those days I found out that he had the most thankful heart I had ever discovered. One day as I struggled with a money problem, trying to come up with enough cash to buy my books at the seminary, he came into my office and he could tell I was troubled. He figured out the problem on his own and opened his wallet and handed me a wad of cash. I backed off, of course. I insisted I could not take his money and that I would figure it out on my own. It was the words that he spoke next that have stayed with me forever . . . "Listen here, young man. Until you learn how to receive, you will never truly understand what it is to give."

It was at that moment that I realized Pastor Malm had such a heart full of gratefulness that he probably needed both those words to express his thankfulness. It always kind of makes me chuckle when I offer prayers of gratitude and I hear myself say those words . . . "Dear Lord . . . we are so THANKFUL and GRATEFUL" . . . there are those days when I find my own heart just overflowing with gratitude.

So I ask you today to sit back and read Psalm 100. It's a Hymn of Praise and no matter what is going on in this world or your own life, it is that psalm that might bring you into a spirit of gratitude . . . *"Enter the temple gates with thanksgiving; go into its courts with praise. Give thanks to him and praise him. The Lord is good; his love is eternal and his faithfulness lasts forever."*

It's a good day to give thanks. Remember to wash your hands, fold them and bow your head. Pause for a bit and see if words of thankfulness fill your heart. Maybe you'll even find yourself saying . . . "Dear Lord, I am so thankful and grateful."

Pray with me: "Our Father, we have so much to be thankful for. Even as we face uncertain times and strange moments. You are by our side as we walk through this life. For your calming presence, for your steady hand . . . we are thankful and grateful. Amen. In Jesus' name, Amen.

THURSDAY, OCTOBER 22, 2020

I am quite sure that most of you reading this have had this very memory: Going to Itasca State Park in northern Minnesota, walking the trail down to the Headwaters of the Mississippi River and then gingerly making your way across those rocks!

Right? I have no idea how small I was the first time I did that. But I clearly remember our children, who were very little at the time, inching their way across those rocks.

And one of our favorite memories was the time they, along with their cousin Gretchen, managed to tumble into the water making for a very soggy ride back home!

We would call out . . . "Be sure to stay on the rocks! Watch your footing!" That's a call out that we would do many times throughout the years. Not necessarily because of the water below, but because of the difficulties and dangers that life hands us.

Jesus is very clear to us about being our rock. We can find that reference over and over again in scripture. And especially in our songs and hymns . . . "Jesus is the Rock in a Weary Land", "How Firm A Foundation" . . . and on and on.

Rocks have special meaning in our spiritual walk. I remember visiting the Jewish graves in Poland and seeing all the stones on the gravestones, signifying the visitors, not just family and friends, but folks who wanted to show that they had been there . . . these people were not forgotten. In fact, we have made it a practice to leave a small stone, a rock, on the gravestones of our parents when we make that pilgrimage to those northern cemeteries.

So what does that say to us today? I think we just need a reminder to keep ourselves focused on **The Rock**. To stand firm in our faith, to keep on building one another up, to have courage, strength and to keep that foundation steady.

I look forward to my next visit to those Headwaters, hopefully with our grandchildren once again. And when I do, I plan to call out . . . 'STAY ON THE ROCKS! WATCH YOUR FOOTING!" and of course, that message will have a much deeper meaning than they could possibly know.

Keep on washing your hands, fold them, bow your head and stay focused. On the Rock.

Pray with me: "Dear Lord, you certainly are our firm foundation. When everything often feels as though it is slipping away you hold us steady. Thanks for that. Help us to be the ones who hold one another up. Amen. In Jesus' Name, Amen.

TUESDAY, OCTOBER 27, 2020

"*For God so loved the world that he gave his only Son, so that everyone who believes in him may not die but have eternal life.*" John 3:16

It's a verse we all learned at a very young age. It says it all. God loved what God created . . . the world and all that is in it. The lakes, the mountains, the plains . . . the creatures . . . even the people. God loved this world so much that God gave up his Son. He did it so that every one who believes in God will live forever.

Sometimes I just don't get this 'world'. And I often wonder what God was thinking! I cannot even begin to imagine giving up my children . . . my grandchildren, for the likes of this world we live in. Dissension, disagreement, name calling, wars and rumors of wars, disrespect for the climate, it seems as though we have found ourselves in quite a mess. And yet . . . God remains in love with our world and all that is in it.

So what can we say? What can we do? I find myself going back to the basic message we find in John 3:16. God loved this world so much . . . and it is our responsibility to care for it, to love it, as well. And how do we do that? It's simple, folks. In spite of all the banners, flags, bumper stickers . . . we remember what God told us through his son, the son God gave up for this world . . . *"YOU ARE TO LOVE YOUR NEIGHBOR . . . JUST AS MUCH AS YOU LOVE YOURSELF."*

Seriously? I should love my neighbor just the way I love myself? I should love my neighbor just the way I love those children, those grandchildren? Yup. It's pretty simple stuff. And I am so simple minded to believe that it can really work. That over the next few days we can put away some of the dissension, the disagreements, and work our way back to the basics. God has laid out a plan for us. The world needs us. The world needs folks like us. The world needs the love God gave when he put his only son upon the earth. The world desperately needs us. Right now.

Please keep washing your hands, fold them and bow your head. Prayer is a powerful tool for us right now. Pray for understanding but most of all pray for a calming presence to come over this world that God loves so much.

Pray with me: "Dear Lord, we have not done a very good job of caring for this beautiful world. Help us to do better. To care for one another a little bit more, to understand more clearly. Help us to be the people who put our world together. Amen. In Jesus' Name, Amen.

THURSDAY, OCTOBER 29, 2020

Have you ever been in the presence of someone who just seems to 'shine'? And when you spend time with them, you go away just feeling so much better about life, about where you are headed? It's almost like starting a day over when that happens.

I have someone in my life like that. I can be down in the dumps, a bit grumpy . . . I hate to admit that . . . and then this friend and I can sit down, in person, or on a call, and I just feel like I have been picked up out of a pit.

Matthew 5:14-16 puts it this way . . . *"You are like a light for the whole world. A city built on a hill cannot be hid. No one lights a lamp and puts it under a bowl; instead he puts it on the lamp-stand, where it gives light for everyone in the house. In the same way your light must shine before people, so that they will see the good things you do and praise your Father in heaven."*

I have heard the saying, "The Christ in me sees the Christ in you" many times. I love it. There are just some people who bring out the Christ in us. And I hope and pray that there are those who can also see the Christ in me.

Our daughter has started a Candlelight vigil in memory of her best friend who committed suicide a number of years ago. It is held annually at Christmas time at a nature center in the Twin Cities. She entitled it "Be the Light". She wanted to find some light in the middle of a very sad and dark time. And we are so very proud of her for honoring her friend this way. And that's what I'm talking about here . . . . let's work on being 'the light' for those who find themselves in dark places. "Let your light so shine" . . . it's a wonderful thought. And we can do it.

Remember washing your hands is essential, then fold them and bow your head. Ask God to help you to light up the dark places. To not hide your light under a bowl, but to let shine and be the Christ someone needs to see in you.

Pray with me: "Dear Lord, sometimes we don't feel as though there is any light in us at all. Help us to discover what we can do and be for those around us. We struggle hard at times and we need your light so desperately. Let us be reflections to those around us of your love and your peace. Amen. In Jesus' Name, Amen.

TUESDAY, NOVEMBER 3

In John 6:35, we read . . . *"I am the bread of life", Jesus told them. "He who comes to me will never be hungry; he who believes in me will never be thirsty."*

When I think of my mother my favorite memory is of her standing over a big bowl kneading bread dough. That woman made the best bread! We talk often of how we loved her bread and her buns! She did that for years in a very small kitchen, just at the kitchen table . . . (no 'island', for sure!), without running water and baking that delicious bread in an old gas stove.

My wife tells of the time she tried to learn my mother's secrets to great bread. She attempted to write down the ingredients and the amounts . . . no luck there! It was a 'pinch' of this and a 'smidgen' of that . . . flour just dumped from that big tin canister. It wasn't that she was trying to keep a big secret . . . she had just been doing it for so long that she knew the 'FEEL' of the dough.

What does that have to do with Jesus telling us He is the Bread of Life? A lot, I think. First of all . . . it's not rocket science. It's the simple Good News. He gives us life giving bread, a model of living without a lot of extra bells and whistles. "Just come to me", he says. "Come to me and you will never be hungry again, you will never thirst."

We have complicated our lives so much. We daily struggle with the hows and the whys of living. We have built walls and barriers around ourselves and each other. We have taken sides and have closed ourselves off in so many ways.

Yes, life was simple back then. Monday was the day to do the washing, Tuesday was the day to bake the bread. Maybe today is the day to step back and just listen once more to the words of Jesus . . . *"Come to me, those of you who are so very hungry . . . believe in me, those who thirst."* This is the Bread of Life, this is our sustenance. This is what keeps us going, keeps us fed, keeps us nourished.

So . . . wash your hands, fold them, bow your head . . . give thanks for the life sustaining love of our Lord, Jesus Christ. And . . . have a good piece of bread today, slather it with some 'real' butter! It is a gift . . . the Bread of Life.

Pray with me: "Dear Lord, thank you for being the nourishment we need during these trying times. Sometimes we are just so hungry, so thirsty and we don't know where to turn to be fed. And there you are . . . in your Word, reminding us that you are what we need. The Bread of Life. Amen. In Jesus' Name, Amen.

THURSDAY, NOVEMBER 5, 2020

One of the things I miss the most during this time of Covid 19 is being unable to visit people in their homes. As a parish pastor, over the years, that was one of my very favorite things to do. We could meet at church, greet one another, have a short visit . . . but going into people's homes was so revealing.

You really get to know one another when you sit together in someone's home. You see what is important to them . . . family photos, mementos, books . . . the way they live on a daily basis. It's a way to seriously make a connection with one another.

A story from my first parish . . . I was invited for 'coffee' at someone's home. Of course, it wasn't just coffee! Sandwiches, fruit salad, cheese, cookies, bars . . . I could go on and on! The dining table was set with the best china. A couple of neighbors were invited to join us. The 'man of the house', the neighbors and myself sat at the table. But Anna never sat down! There wasn't even a chair set for her. She poured coffee, fussed over the food, hustled back and forth from the kitchen. Finally, I couldn't take it anymore! I said, "Anna, please sit down and join us!" Her reply . . . "Oh no . . . I am just here to serve."

I'm not sure that wonderful lady realized what she was demonstrating. Her entire life had been one of service. She served at church . . . she served her family and her community . . . she was a servant, for sure. But there is more to that story. She was a wonderful musician, had a career in public education, served on various boards and committees. Her home was a welcoming place for all kinds of people. She got it. She never really quit being a servant . . . right up to the very end.

Service is all about making a connection. Jesus shows us in Luke 22:26 . . . *"But this is not the way it is with you; rather, the greatest one among you must be like the youngest, and the leader must be like the servant."* Loving our neighbor like we love ourselves often begins with SERVICE. Leaving the 'high altar' where we sometimes find ourselves and going out . . . where the people are, finding them in their comfortable places, and sometimes in their 'uncomfortable' places, and then connecting . . . serving one another.

I look forward to the day when we can sit together at the table . . . maybe in our homes or maybe at the table here in church. Until that day is safe . . . continue to wash your hands, fold them, bow your head and pray for one another.

Pray with me: "Dear Lord, you taught us what it is to be a servant. Help us to be the servant church. To lift one another up when we are down, to love one another through all times and difficulties. Let us continue to find ways to serve you . . . and one another. Amen. In Jesus' Name, Amen.

TUESDAY, NOVEMBER 10, 2020

Remember teaching a child how to ride a bike? I can remember so well hanging on to the back of the bike and hearing "Dad! Don't let go!" "Dad! Please don't let go!" Well, you know the story . . . eventually, you just **have** to let go. Sometimes they don't even realize you're not still there! And then . . . Voila! Off they go, on their own!

It's a fond memory, for sure. In Proverbs 4, we read . . . *"Look straight ahead with honest confidence . . . Plan carefully what you do, and whatever you do will turn out right . . . . walk straight ahead, don't go one step off the way."*

Back in those 'bike ride teaching days', wouldn't you have just loved to add those wise words? Just stay straight ahead . . . keep your focus and whatever you do will be the right thing as long as you stay on the path.

It doesn't always go like that. But I think today is a good day to 're-focus', don't you? Let's think about moving forward. Sometimes we aren't so sure where that path will take us but with God's good guidance we move ahead.

In the 'work world', we would frequently hear the words . . . . "Going forward". In other words, it's time to forget the mistakes of the past and move forward. Staying steady is not always so easy but it is so important . . . . In life, as well as on the bike! At this point in our living, we sometimes find ourselves focusing, or speaking about . . . our past. We may not see much ahead. But that is not what our God calls us to do. God reminds us over and over in scripture that we always have work to do. We just may need to 're-focus' how to get the job done.

We find ourselves still struggling and wondering what comes next with the corona virus and our nation. Let's remind ourselves to take good care of one another . . . and our own selves. Please keep focused . . . wash your hands, fold them, bow your head and ask God to help you/me focus once again on the path that lies before us.

Pray with me: "Dear Lord, inspire me this day to see what lies ahead . . . and leave behind the mistakes of the past. Keep us steady on the path, keep us balanced and focused. Give strength to those who are caregivers during these days. Amen. In Jesus' Name, Amen.

THURSDAY, NOVEMBER 12, 2020

Psalm 51:10 .... *"Create a pure heart in me, O God, and renew a right spirit within me."*

How do I go about purifying my heart? I know one thing . . . at our house the fine aroma of Lysol, bleach, cleanser, sanitizer has filled the air. During this time of Coronavirus, it seems like we just can't be sure that everything we touch is REALLY clean!

So the house is fine. But my heart? I'm not always so sure. It seems like it accumulates a great deal of 'garbage' these days. Garbage days at our house are Monday and Thursday. We have a great big garbage can . . . for just the two of us. When I wheel it back to the house on Monday afternoon I often think . . . "Well, good! All the garbage is gone!" And then on Thursday, when I wheel it back out to the curb, what do you know? It's full of more garbarge!

That's kind of how it is for us, isn't it? When we ask God to 'create a clean, a pure heart within us', we should be good, don't you think? We confess our sins, ask for that cleansing part . . . and then, before you know it, our hearts are all filled up with 'junk' once more.

It's an ongoing process. Some days I'd like to just take that big bottle of Dawn soap and scrub my heart clean. That should do it! That stuff is powerful! But I can't. So I pull up all the TRUST I can muster. I trust that as I confess what it is that muddies up my life God has the cleansing power to create that pure heart within me. Yes, even me.

And I really believe that God can do that for us, all of us. And especially our nation as we move through this process we find ourselves in. We need a Heart Cleansing. We need to confess what it is that has torn us apart, forgive one another and then create a new spirit among us. It can happen. Sometimes it happens just one act at a time . . . one person at a time. But it can happen.

Please keep on washing your hands, fold them, bow your head and ask God to create that brand new loving heart within each of us.

Pray with me: "Dear God, we pray for the power of your Holy Spirit to move within each of us and across our land, our globe. We need your heart cleansing. Amen. In Jesus's Name, Amen.

TUESDAY, NOVEMBER 17, 2020

Ever since last March when we started 'staying at home' so much, I have been doing more reading than I did since my student days. I believe I have shared with you before that sometimes I like to 'peek' at the end of the book . . . admitedly, I cheat . . . sometimes I really want to know how it's going to 'come out' before investing in the whole story!

Aren't we all a little like that? We'd really like to know the outcome before we start something new. I like the saying . . . *"You grow only by coming to the end of something and by beginning something else."*

Reflecting on beginnings and endings I can't help but think of the words we know so well . . . **I AM. I AM THE ALPHA AND THE OMEGA. I AM THE BEGINNING AND THE END.** In Isaiah 44:6, we read: *"The Lord, who rules and protects Israel, the Lord Almighty, has this to say: 'I am the first, the last, the only God; there is no other God but me.'"*

I really like knowing that God was with me in my very beginning and God will be with me at the very end. What happens in the middle has its ups and downs. There have been many joys and sorrows in this 'in between' time but it has not been a journey without the accompaniment of that God who met me in my baptism.

I find so much comfort in that these days. I don't really need to 'peek' ahead to see what's coming at the end. I know the end of the story. God will be there for me (and for you) enveloping us in God's comforting arms. Like we sing in that great hymn . . . *"I was there to hear your borning cry . . . I'll be there to guide you through the night when your life is done."*

No, these days are not easy days. We have so much uncertainty. But we faithfully follow the One who is the Beginning and is the End. And on the road between those two points we trust each day, doing what God has reminded us needs to be done. Loving one another, caring for all and completing the work God has called us to do.

Please wash your hands, fold them, bow your head and focus on what can be done each day to make life better for yourself and others.

Pray with me: "Heavenly Father, thank you for being there for us as we travel these roads. We trust our lives to you. Amen. In Jesus' Name, Amen.

E-DEVOTION FOR
NOVEMBER 19

Some time back I wrote a devotional thought about our orange tree. Some of you may remember that you gave me advice on how to 'prod' the tree into producing oranges. At that time I mentioned we got 6 oranges from it.

Well, I took all the advice. I even WHACKED it a couple of times with a big stick! (Thanks for that tip!)

So . . . I suppose you're imagining us enjoying fresh squeezed OJ from our tree, right? WRONG. We search and search for oranges . . . and good news. WE HAVE ONE OR-ANGE. We can't wait to pick it and enjoy sharing it.

We're keeping the tree, of course. We know that next year will be a better year. (This is 2020, of course. It figures.)

This experience took me to Romans 8:25 . . . *"But if we hope for what we do not see, we wait for it with patience."* I have hope and patience that our orange tree will certainly produce some fruit for us next year.

It makes we think about how impatient I have been about so much. Especially this virus. I want it over! I want it gone! I want my life back! How about you? And then we find ourselves reminded that God is so patient with us. As this chapter in Romans tells us..God keeps coming to us in our weakness, helps us when we don't know how to pray, God sees the good that is in us and in all things works through us to do what it is that needs to be done, according to His plan.

So . . . I'll just keep checking my orange tree, and you keep washing your hands, fold them . . . take a look at your thumbs in the shape of the cross, bow your head and give thanks that God is patient with us as we grow and produce.

Pray with me: "Dear Lord, thank you for sticking with me. Even when I don't produce much fruit. Help me to be patient with others, to show love and compassion. Strengthen those who care for the sick and dying. Grant us all a greater degree of understanding. Amen. In Jesus' Name, Amen.

TUESDAY, NOVEMBER 23, 2020

Well . . . here we are! Thanksgiving week. Feeling thankful (and grateful!)? If you are like me, you may have to dig deep to discover thankfulness right now. There's a lot going on for all of us.

We're thankful we finally found a Butterball turkey that wasn''t TOO big or TOO small for just the two of us! Oh yes . . . we plan to spend Thanksgiving Day as we usually do . . . turkey, dressing, sweet potatoes, green beans, mashed potatoes, gravy..etc. For JUST US? Well, we will share a large platter each, for Toby and Joel, our neighbors.

But it will be just us this year. And as I search my soul for some thankfulness, I am indeed, grateful that we can share in that meal.

I watched a segment on a Sunday morning show this weekend . . . it was about the long food lines, the stressed food banks, the people who never in a million years thought they would be standing in a line for food for their family.

So I am . . . THANKFUL AND GRATEFUL. And I am sure, as you do a little soul searching yourselves . . . you are, as well.

I think of Luke 12:22 . . . . *"And Jesus said, 'Do no worry about the food you need to stay alive or the clothes you need for your body . . . life is much more than food, clothes"* . . . . that's a hard text to share with folks standing in breadlines, isn't it? What can we do about these things? Be grateful for what we have and then go about God's work sharing our blessings, our food, our goods, our bounty with those who find themselves worrying this Thanksgiving.

Have faith, folks. Sometimes it is difficult and the way is weary. But our Father assures us again and again . . . in verse 32 . . . "Do not be afraid, little flock, for your Father is pleased to give you the Kingdom" . . . and verse 34 . . . "For your heart will always be where your riches are."

It may be a time for soul searching to discover what it is we are thankful for . . . and continue to wear a mask, wash your hands, fold them, bow your head and dig up a prayer of thanksgiving.

Pray with me: "Dear Lord, we give you thanks for all we have been given. Help us to find ways to share our bounty . . . our lives, with all people. Grant to us compassionate hearts and caring souls. Give us willing hands to get the work done you have asked us to do. Amen. In Jesus's Name, Amen.

THURSDAY, NOVEMBER 26, THANKSGIVING DAY, 2020

Many families have the tradition of going around the Thanksgiving dinner table and one by one stating what each person is thankful for that year.

I remember doing that when I was small and having that panicky feeling . . . "What should I say?" It's kind of like trying to come up with a Jeopardy answer that won't illustrate how 'dumb' you really are!

So . . . I decided today, Thanksgiving Day, 2020 I should share with you what it is that makes my heart swell with gratitude today.

Here we go:

Faith. I'm so thankful that my faith is still sustaining me. Even after all these years and the many questions I have troubled God with in my moments of doubt. FAITH. I guess that's my number 1.

Family. We're sure not the "Perfect Family". We've had our struggles and our pains. But I am so grateful that after 54 years my wife still tolerates my many quirks, my bad habits, my 'weirdness'. And my children . . . my grandchildren. I often wonder if they know how much they are loved by their father? Their grandfather?

Work. I've had the pleasure of sharing my faith and my life with people who were receptive to the Gospel these many years. I think back of all those good souls who fed me and loved me and listened to me, even when I wasn't all that sure of what I was saying.

Life. The idea that God gives me one more day to be God's servant in this world. The sunrise as I face each day and the sunset as it comes to end.

There's more, of course. But today . . . Thanksgiving, 2020 . . . take time to tell one another and God what it is that has filled your heart with gratitude.

And wear a mask. Wash your hands, fold them and bow your head. Give Thanks.

> *Give thanks with a grateful heart*
> *Give thanks to the Holy One*
> *Give thanks because He's given Jesus Christ, His Son*
> *Give thanks with a grateful heart*
> *Give thanks to the Holy One*
> *Give thanks because He's given Jesus Christ, His Son*
> *And now let the weak say, "I am strong"*
> *Let the poor say, "I am rich*
> *Because of what the Lord has done for us"*
> *And now let the weak say, "I am strong"*
> *Let the poor say, "I am rich*
> *Because of what the Lord has done for us"*
> *Give thanks with a grateful heart (with a grateful heart)*
> *Give thanks to the Holy One (to the Holy One)*
> *Give thanks because He's given Jesus Christ, His Son*
> *Give thanks with a grateful heart (with a grateful heart)*
> *Give thanks to the Holy One (to the Holy One)*
> *Give thanks because He's given Jesus Christ, His Son*
> *And now let the weak say, "I am strong"*
> *Let the poor say, "I am rich*
> *Because of what the Lord has done for us"*
> *And now let the weak say, "I am strong"*

Let the poor say, "I am rich (I am rich)
Because of what the Lord has done for us"
Give thanks

HAPPY THANKSGIVING!

TUESDAY, DECEMBER 1

"Hail, O Favored One! The Lord is with you . . . blessed are you!"

That is the message of Advent One. Our first week of Advent before the birth of the Christchild once again.

Have you ever felt 'favored'? Growing up I always heard from my sister and brother and cousins . . . "Oh sure . . . you get this or that . . . just because you are Grampa's and Gramma's FAVORITE!

Was I? I doubt it. I think they loved us all the same. But there were times . . . when I was sure that I **was** the 'favored' one. And it made me feel pretty wonderful.

Having had three children I am sure there were occasions with them, as well, when one felt that the other was more 'favored' than they were. But of course, that wasn't true. We love and loved them all the same.

Being favored by God is a pretty wonderful feeling. If you go into Luke and read the first chapter you will come upon those words. God showed favoritism! God sent an angel to this young teenager and she found herself in quite a predicament! She was pregnant . . . and not married! That doesn't seem to be a situation where you are 'favored', does it? But the angel went on with the words . . . "Peace be with you. The Lord is with you and has greatly blessed you!"

What a great message from God for these days. We are all FAVORED! God doesn't just pick out the smartest, or the most talented, or the wisest or even the richest for God's favoritism. God comes to you and to me in the Advent message for this time. And God reminds us that no matter who we are, or how 'less than' we feel . . . we are God's favorite! And then through God's angels, (and remember . . . you never know 'who' they are), God tells us that Peace is upon us. Our present struggles are in God's hands. "The Lord has greatly blessed us" and no matter what comes our way . . . God is with us.

So with that thought in mind . . . please wear a mask, continue to wash your hands, fold them and bow your heads. Remember . . . YOU are God's favorite!

Pray with me: "Dear Lord, we live each day, each moment in holy anticipation. We ask for your peace to find it's way into the lives of many who are sick, those who are weary of working, those who don't know where the next dollar will come from. Inspire and enliven us to be your angels doing your business in this world. Give us power . . . give us strength . . . give us peace." Amen, In Jesus's Name, Amen.

THURSDAY, DECEMBER 3, 2020

"The angel said to her, 'Don't be afraid, Mary. God has been gracious to you."

I love the song, "Be Not Afraid". The words speak to me of a time of transition. Moving from one, probably 'comfortable' place to a new experience. I have heard that it is a song that is often sung on death row as someone is on that journey.

Going on in our Advent walk we discover the angel is still with Mary. She has just been told that she is the 'favored' one. It's startling for her to have this visit from the angel. I think we all would be equally alarmed! But the angel says those comforting words . . . *"Don't be afraid".*

The words of the song, Be Not Afraid, go like this: "Be not afraid, I go before you always. Come follow me and I will give you rest."

Have you ever found yourself truly afraid? I have. As a child, I was afraid of the dark. I remember having to cross the yard to the barn on a dark night . . . no stars, no moon. And then realizing that my father was walking ahead of me and even though I could barely see his figure, I could follow him.

We're going through some uncharted waters this Advent. Some are finding that Christmas may not be at all as they imagined. Some are 'afraid' of that big, ugly virus that just seems to keep moving around us. Some are afraid that life as we knew it may never be the same again.

And then this Advent message comes to us . . . *"Don't be*

afraid! God has been gracious to you." This God who sends the angel is the God who goes before us and is with us each and every day, giving us comfort. We are not alone. Just as God sent that angel to Mary with those words . . . God sends angels to us each and every day to carry us on our journey. So, follow Mary's lead . . . even though the questions loom before us . . . we are not afraid.

Take time on your Advent walk this year to read the story in Luke over and over again and you too, will find yourself strengthened and empowered . . . just as Mary did.

By the way . . . wear a mask. Wash your hands, fold them and bow your head. Give thanks. And BE NOT AFRAID.

Pray with me: "Dear Lord, we are so grateful for your presence. Just as Mary found the courage to face the unknown, we too, find that same courage. Let us look for the angels among us and . . . better yet, let us BE the angels for others." Amen. In Jesus's Name, Amen.

TUESDAY, DECEMBER 8, 2020

As I have been reflecting on the announcement Gospel of Luke, I find myself once again thinking about Mary. I really like the Christmas song . . . "Mary, Did You Know?" And I wonder . . . What did Mary know? Not much, it seems. It says in Luke, chapter 1:30 . . . *"The angel said to her, 'Don't be afraid, Mary. God has been gracious to you."*

So Mary did know that God was with her. Beyond that, I really don't think she had a clue about what was about to happen. Did she know, as the song says . . . "That your baby boy would give sight to the blind? That he will calm a storm with just his hand? That because of this child, the deaf will hear, the lame will leap and this child is the great I AM?"

No. I don't think so. She just trusted in what the angel had to say.

I don't think I know so much, anymore. As a young seminary student I thought I really knew it all! I could see the future . . . and man, it looked great! And then . . . life happened. Many of our plans fall apart. Even this Christmas. It doesn't look like it is turning out the way we wanted it to. For most of us our dreams of sharing the Christmas Story with our children and our grandchildren just may not happen. Not in person, anyway.

And I KNOW this . . . 'virtual' visits really don't cut it with me! I want the 'skin on' kind of visit. I KNOW that!

And then . . . I am reminded that the story of Advent . . . the promise of Christmas is a very, very 'SKIN ON' kind of event! Jesus came into this world . . . my world and yours . . . with skin on. There was nothing 'virtual' about that experience. I KNOW an angel really, really did visit Mary. And I KNOW that she became pregnant with the Son of God. And I KNOW that no matter where this Christmas takes me . . . I can spend these Advent days getting my heart (and my questioning mind) prepared for this amazing birth.

Please take time to read the story in Luke. Think about Mary . . . and what she DID NOT know, and yet believed. And wear a mask. Wash your hands, fold them, bow your head and prepare your heart for something powerful . . . something we KNOW is going to happen!

Pray with me: "Dear Lord, these Advent days are days for us to 'get ready'. Some of us are not getting ready to see family, we may not be getting ready for company, we may not even be getting ready to worship together. But lift us out of our times of doubt . . . keep us focused on the one truth . . . that we KNOW. Your Son is coming once again. Help us to be ready. Amen. In Jesus' Name, Amen.

THURSDAY, DECEMBER 10, 2020

I am still stuck in Luke and thinking about Mary. After the angel told Mary all these things that she probably could not understand, her response was simple . . . Luke 1:38 . . . *"I am the Lord's servant, may it happen to me as you have said."*

And then what cosmic event happened? THE ANGEL LEFT HER! Oh great. Have you ever had someone come and tell you something that was just amazing, unbelivable . . . and then simply turn around and WALK AWAY?

Good grief. It's like if they came to your door and said . . . "Guess what? You just won the Publisher's Clearing House prize money! One million dollars! And then . . . poof! Gone. What would you do?

Well, I would stand there for quite some time. Not being able to believe what just happened. (And then, of course . . . I'd go deposit the check!)

What did Mary do? We really don't know exactly what she did at the first precise moment, but shortly . . . she ran off to share the Good News with her cousin, Elizabeth. Good news is meant to be shared! When something wonderful happens usually the first thing I do is call someone. I just cannot keep it to myself! So that's what Mary did. She believed what the angel told her was really, truly going to happen. She couldn't' understand HOW it was going to happen, but she knew this message from the angel was, in fact, directly from God. And so she ran to someone she trusted and she shared the news. It was too good to keep to herself.

That's part of the Advent message. Not only are we in 'preparation' mode, it's time for us to spread the word! Like the song says . . . "Go, Tell it on the Mountain!" Shout it from the rooftops . . . tell your neighbors . . . pass it on. These aren't just days of baking, wrapping, shopping . . . these are the days to get the word out!

This is actually . . . the BEST NEWS OF ALL! In just a few short weeks we are going to be sitting beside the manger, in the stable . . . worshipping the Newborn Child. And we can do that from anywhere! Because this baby is not confined to any one place. His birth reaches around the world . . . into every home. That's BIG NEWS. Let's get busy sharing it!

Wear a mask. Wash your hands, fold them and bow your head. The time is almost here! Give God the glory for this good news!

Pray with me: "Dear Lord, give us the courage to share this Great News . . . with everyone, everywhere. For Christ is coming! He is here! Amen, In Jesus' Name, Amen.

In Luke chapter 1, the story is told of Mary going to share her good news with her cousin, Elizabeth. Elizabeth was also pregnant and in time she gave birth to a son. When people asked her what this new baby's name was going to be . . . she said, "His name is John." Everyone was puzzled as they had no relatives with such a name . . . naming a child something other than a 'family' name was unpredictable. When the people turned to the baby's father, Zacheriah to question this strange decision, he wrote on a piece of paper . . . HIS NAME IS JOHN. It was after that, Zacheriah was able to speak once more.

Unpredictable! That's what this Advent has been for most of us. We are living in a very 'unexpected' time. I was thinking about that and I remembered years ago when we had a Sunday School program in my first parish. As 'predicted' the program ended with the Nativity scene. The characters came up the aisle . . . first the angels, then the shepherds . . . the Holy Family . . . followed by the kings.

That year the congregation saw something 'unexpected'. The Sunday School superintendent had gone out on a limb and asked the children what part they wanted to play in the Nativity. A little curly headed fellow said . . . "I really want to be an angel!" (Now, in this place . . . a boy had never played the angel before). "No problem" . . . was the answer. Then little Cynthia said . . . "I want to be a shepherd!" Oh Oh . . . that was really 'unpredictable'! And to top it off, Marilyn decided she should be a KING! They all played their parts beautfully. But it was a Nativity Scene we had not experienced before.

That's how this Advent is shaping up for me. I'm finding myself in an unpredictable mode of preparation. And that's ok. Maybe taking ourselves 'outside the norm' isn't such a bad thing.

I have such great hope for our church, our country and our world during this Advent season. I am hoping and praying that we can reach outside our normal selves and see things a little differently. After all . . . that's what this newborn child did. This child came into our world and set about doing things in a very 'unpredictable' way. We can too.

Wear your mask. Wash your hands, fold them and bow your heads. Pray for understanding and acceptance in this unpredictable time.

Pray with me: "Dear Lord, thank you for accepting us just as we are. Help us to show that same acceptance with one another. Fill our hearts with love, our souls with peace as we make ourselves ready this Advent. Amen. In Jesus' Name, Amen.

DECEMBER 17, 2020

In Luke, chapter 2 we read about the journey Joseph and Mary took from Nazareth, their home town, to Bethlehem. We have all speculated on what a trip that had to be! Young, pregnant girl . . . sitting on donkey, over some rough terrain.

You may have heard me tell this before . . . whenever we take a car trip I usually like to start out about 3-4 hours before we had really planned to leave. I want to get a headstart! And then, I'll calculate just how many hours we can go before my eyes are so tired I can't see the road ahead. I'm usually just FOCUSED on the end of the day! The END of the trip! My wife often comments . . . "Can't you just enjoy the journey instead of always thinking of the destination?"

That's just my nature, I guess. I've been wondering about Joseph. How do you think he felt taking off from Narareth? He knew he had no choice, he had to register for the taxation. Somehow I imagine he may have been a little like me . . . let's just GET THERE! There probably wasn't a great deal of gorgeous scenery to enjoy, anyway. He must have felt the terrible weight of responsibility for this young woman and the unborn child.

So . . . here we are! Advent IV just ahead! We're almost at the destination. Christmas is just one week away. And, true to nature . . . I find myself concentrating on December 24th and 25th. Whoa! I think I'm going to take a break. I think I'm going to just try to stay focused on this part of the journey. My heart needs a little work to find room for that Christmas event.

Pause . . . picture that little family. Plodding along on their trip. Uncomfortable? I am sure. Not what they had hoped and planned for? Absolutely. But there they are . . . one step after another. That is how we can find ourselves these last days of our Advent journey. One step at a time.

While you're on this last leg of the journey, wear a mask. Wash your hands, fold them . . . picture that cross with your thumbs . . . bow your heads, pray for not only the destination . . . but for courage while we continue on the way.

Pray with me: "Dear Lord, we find ourselves impatient on this journey. We want the end to come. But we know we live in your time, not our own. Give us courage as we go these last miles . . . give us patience. Give us peace. Amen. In Jesus' Name, Amen"

TUESDAY, DECEMBER 22, 2020

Today I find myself hearing the words.."Unto us, a Child is born" over and over in my head. And so it was . . . and so it will be.

It was an exciting time when we had the chance to announce that a child was born! We had a couple of different experiences with that event. When our first child was born I didn't make it in time! That kid just didn't wait for me. When our second child was born neither one of us were at the birth. But I remember vividly the day that three week old little girl was placed in our arms and we were amazed at what a gift we had been given. And then, came number three . . . I was a real trouper and even though I was close to passing out, I was there for every moment! Each of those events, unique as they are, are treasured memories.

A friend sent us a picture of those three taken with Santa Claus about 42-43 years ago. She had come across it in her mother's things following her passing. I've looked at that old photo many times these last couple of days. I realized something. When I see those children now, grown adults . . . I still see those little ones. Unto us . . . a child is given. Once a child . . . always a child.

What did it take for God to present us with the only child God ever had? Love . . . the greatest love known to humankind. And not only did God give us this child, born of a young woman, in a stable . . . God gave this child up for us. On a cross.

That love I felt as a parent 45-52 years ago when I first laid my eyes on that small baby, that's the same love I feel for each one of those children yet today. Just as God sees us as God's own child . . . each one of us unique, created in God's own image.

Yes, Christmas is different this year in so many ways. But the simple truth remains. God loved us so much that God gave us God's only Son. Born in a manger, in a stable of a poor working class couple. Enjoy your memories this year. Recall all the Christmases that have gone by and then look forward to the many Christmases yet to come.

Wear a mask. Wash your hands. Fold them, bow your heads and give God thanks for all the memories.

Pray with me: "Dear Lord, help us to stay focused on the manger. On the stable. On the little family and on the Christchild. Thank you for all those Christmases we have shared, keep us strong as we show our love one to the other. Amen. In Jesus' Name, Amen.

THURSDAY, DECEMBER 24, 2020

And here we are! Christmas Eve, 2020! Merry Christmas!

In college I sang in The Messiah..grant it, I didn't have a major part as I'm really not much of a singer. But the choir director invited any student who was interested to sing with the choir. I jumped at the chance. It was thrilling! What I remember the most is this . . .

"And His name shall be called..WONDERFUL! COUNSELOR! THE PRINCE OF PEACE!"

I remember singing those words at the top of my lungs. And HE is just that! He is Wonderful, He is our Counselor . . . He is the Prince of Peace!

After the events of this past year I need a counselor! There have been times in many of our lives when a counselor was really necessary. Maybe struggles in a marriage, troubled teens, frustrations with work, substance abuse, depression . . . those are the times when having someone to 'go' to, to talk with, to gleen some advice are very important.

It's hard to admit we can't do it alone. It takes a lot of strength to ask for help . . . to look for a counselor. And yet . . . here we are! Christmas Eve and our Counselor is born! This is the Christchild who is here to walk with us every step of the way, through our lonely times, through our despair and through our difficulties. What Great News!

I'm asking you to 'ask Alexa', or tune into the radio, maybe even find an old record of Handel's Messiah this Christmas. The words are so powerful. The music so inspiring. This is the day, the night, to let those words run back and forth through our minds. No matter what happens we are definitely NOT alone this Christmas! Our Counselor is born! The Prince who brings us peace is here.

Whether we worship in a church or online sitting at home please know that we are very much 'together'. We are joined in a circle around the manger. One family. And we have our Counselor . . . the Prince of Peace right there in the middle of us.

Wear a mask. Wash your hands, fold them and bow your heads. Let those words "Wonderful . . . Counselor . . . Prince of Peace" be in your minds and in your hearts this Christmas.

Pray with me: "Dear Lord, what can we say to thank you for this . . . the Greatest Gift of all? We worship you, we praise you . . . fill our minds with peace, our hearts with love. Amen.

In Jesus' Name, Amen.

TUESDAY, DECEMBER 29, 2020

James is a very small book in the Bible. It will only take you a short time to read through it. I encourage you to do that as we close out this year, 2020. It has a great deal of practical wisdom and simple advise.

I hit on James 4:13-15 . . . "Now listen to me, you that say . . . 'Today or tomorrow we will travel to a certain city, where we will stay a year and go into business and make a lot of money." You don't even know what your life tomorrow will be! You are like a puff of smoke which appears for a moment and then disappears. What you should say is this: "If the Lord is willing we will live and do this or that."

Boy! I wish I would have read those words at the close of 2019! Because I had all kinds of ideas as to what I would do, where I would go in the year 2020. Didn't work out as I had planned. And I'm a 'planner'. As I have said before, I write a 'to do' list every day. Even if I have almost nothing to do.

Some translations use "you are but a wisp of fog" instead of "you are like a puff of smoke". I like both of those illustrations. You know how quickly a wisp of fog can pass us by. And also how fast a puff of smoke can disappear.

It's kind of humilitating, isn't it? Especially when we see ourselves as indespensible, so self important? We really are just 'here today and gone tomorrow'. So what good is it to plan? I still think making plans is important. We sat drinking our coffee just this morning, planning on how soon we can visit our family again. But James reminds us that it is not in our planning but in our realization that we are not the ones in control. So now, I remind myself to silently say . . . "If the Lord is willing . . . I will do this or that."

We've learned a great deal about giving up control this past year. The virus really has a lot more to say about where we go and what we do . . . than we do. Read on in James . . . especially the final chapter. We are reminded to be patient and to keep our hopes high. Some good advise for these last days of 2020.

Wear a mask. Wash your hands, fold them and bow your heads. Ask God for direction, for patience. These days are nothing but a wisp of fog. They are nothing but a puff of smoke.

Pray with me: "Dear Lord, so often I want MY will to be done instead of YOUR will. Remind me to let go. Give me courage to face each and every day with patience. Amen. In Jesus' Name, Amen.

THURSDAY, DECEMBER 31, 2020

GOODBYE 2020! Doesn't that feel good? This is a year we are happy to close the book on. This is the year I am ready to throw the calendar in the trash!

I'm usually not too good with 'goodbyes' but this time . . . GO AWAY! I am done with you!

If you grew up in the midwest as I did, you probably remember saying goodbye to friends or relatives following a visit. It usually started with . . . "We should go now." "Oh, not yet! Let's have another cup of coffee". Then the ritual would begin . . . finding the coats, easing out of the door, standing on the porch for at least 20 minutes, ambling over to the car, another 10-15 minutes of conversation. Then into the car . . . finally slowing back out of the driveway. We always call it . . . "The Long North Dakota/Minnesota Goodbye".

We just didn't master the art of saying goodbye. I never have. It just seems so final. So 'done'. I don't like it. I like to savor the moment . . . keep the conversation going.

But today! Give it up. This year has been hard on so many. So much loss. So much confusion. So much despair. I am glad to see it go.

And I am so excited to open my calendar book tomorrow and start brand new. But I do think we need to pause a bit and say a 'long goodbye' to 2020. We've learned so much. And I have such hope that in 2021 we will find ourselves a bit more understanding because of what we have experienced. I have hopes for more kindness, more compassion, more love for one another.

And so I can only share with you the words I have come to love so much . . . My gift for the close of 2020 . . . The Priestly Blessing:

"The Lord bless you and keep you, The Lord be kind and gracious to you,

May the Lord look upon you with favor and give you peace."

In the Name of the Father, the Son, and the Holy Spirit.
Amen.

Wash your hands, fold them, bow your heads. Give thanks for where we have been and where we are going. And please get the vaccine when it is available to you.

Pray with me: "Thank you Lord, for another year of grace. Give us faithful hearts as we face the year ahead. Bring us together as your people, your church, our nation and our world. We continue our prayers for those who care for the sick, the injured, the lonely and the hungry. Open our hearts to do for others as we would have others do for us." Amen. In Jesus' Name, Amen.

Happy New Year!

JANUARY 5, 2021

I looked up the meaning of the word RESOLVE. It says "to decide firmly on a course of action". Why would I even bother to do that? Well, of course . . . because I have made a few 'Resolutions' for this new year.

We were only 2 days in and I broke the first one. Now . . . here we are 5 days in and I am 'standing firm'. I AM going to exercise more this year! I AM going to eat less! I WILL lose those extra pounds.

I am standing firm in my RESOLVE. I do it every year. And by about mid-January I find myself just losing ground. I tried to find some help in Scripture . . . there were a few verses I could apply here but the one I settled on is in I Corinthians 15, verse 58: *"So then, my dear brothers (and sisters), stand firm and steady."*

Good advice, for sure. As we opened the calendar for 2021 there were nothing but empty spaces. I 'resolved' to fill those days with good work! Not to waste a single moment on unnecessary worries or frustrations. We had enough of that last year. I have 'resolved' to start each day with a prayer for the right attitude . . . positive thoughts . . . a smile . . . an open heart . . . a loving spirit.

I'm probably not being very realistic, am I? Surely, there will be some hard times in this year, as well. More than likely I'll come home one day with a scowl on my face and a 'stinking' attitude. We are only human, right?

So what are we to do as we begin a year with all kinds of new possibilities? Be realistic, sure. But also . . . let's 'resolve' to make more of an effort to do what Jesus tells us to do . . . "Love our neighbor the way we love ourself". As I feel so good about where I am headed this year . . . I do love myself. But that's not enough, we are reminded. Let's make a genuine effort to show understanding, compassion, love to all people.

We're putting some tough times behind us. I really think . . . no, I KNOW . . . it's time to RESOLVE to do a better job at living together. In our homes, our neighborhoods, our communities, our churches . . . for sure, in our nation . . . and in our world.

It's time to RESOLVE to do better.

Keep on washing your hands, fold them, bow your heads, ask God for help in resolving to be better. And get that vaccine when you can.

Pray with me: "Dear Lord, I need to work harder at loving my neighbor. Even the ones I don't like very much, don't agree with. You are the One who told us how to do these difficult things. Give us strength to do what needs to get done this new year. Amen. In Jesus' Name, Amen.

THURSDAY, JANUARY 7, 2021

I must be honest here . . . I had a devotional thought written for this day. Sometimes I write these thoughts a day or two ahead, just to stay 'organized'.

But as I watched the events unfold yesterday at our United States Capitol buiilding, I found myself becoming troubled about what it was I could share that would ease our minds or calm our spirits. It was hard to watch.

I turned to Isaiah. The book of Isaiah tells of a time of unrest, lack of trust and discord. Isaiah did not disappoint. In the very first chapter I came across these words:

"Come now, let us reason together", says the Lord.
Though your sins are as scarlet, they will be white as snow."

The words that caught me were . . . **"COME, LET US REASON TOGETHER"**. Isaiah is telling us clearly that the time has come for us to come together. The time has come to reason together. Some translations reveal those words as "Come, let us bring our disputes to an end."

I like that thought. It definitely is the time for disputes to end, reason and trust to take their place. We are so much better than what we witnessed in our nation yesterday.

So what can we say of these things? I guess it's pretty simple . . . the time has come for us to come together, to put our disputes to an end. As the church . . . the Family of God . . . we are the peacemakers. Let's start by making peace with one another. And praying and working for peace in our nation and this world.

Wear a mask . . . wash your hands, fold them and bow your heads. There is so much to pray for. Ask God to lead us, each and every one . . . *to reason together and put our disputes to an end.*

Pray with me: "Dear Lord, we need your guidance. As your people, as your church and as our nation. We ask for courage to 'turn the other cheek', to forgive, but most of all to find a way to put our differences aside and unite. Unite as a church. Unite as a nation. **We are your hands and feet in this world**. Give us guidance." Amen. In Jesus' Name, Amen.

TUESDAY, JANUARY 12, 2021

As I sat down to write this devotional for this day, I was at a loss. I had no words. So, I did what I often do when I find myself in that state, I opened my Bible and there it was . . . Matthew 8:23-26:

> *"Jesus got into a boat, and his disciples went with him. Suddenly a fierce storm hit the lake, and the boat was in danger of sinking. Jesus was asleep . . . the disciples woke him saying, 'Save us Lord! We are about to die!' Jesus answered them, 'What little faith you have!' Then he got up and ordered the winds and the waves to stop, and there was great calm."*

It feels like we are in the middle of a great storm. Many of us have faced fierce storms before in life. We just want to WAKE UP find the winds have died down and the waves are calm . . . smooth sailing . . . . straight ahead.

I pray that day is coming. I hope so. What will it take? The message comes to us clearly in verse 26 . . . "What little faith you have". My faith has been shaken more than once in this lifetime and I would suppose yours has, as well. Faith in fellow humans, faith in institutions, faith in the church, faith in our nation. But the one thing that has always held true is that there is a Presence with us in these storms of life that has the power to 'calm' the waters.

This is the day the Lord has made. It is the day to shore up our faith. It is the day to turn to the Almighty God and ask for what it is we, each one, can do to calm this storm. Because I really believe we have the power within us to do just that. We are the People of God, we bear His Holy Name . . . settle down in the boat! Be a calming influence in this lifetime. Good Lord, we surely need it.

And wear a mask, wash your hands, fold them and bow your heads. Ask for guidance to help calm these waters. Let's get this storm behind us.

Pray with me: "Dear Lord, we are in such dire need of your calming presence. Open our hearts and our minds to do what it is that You would have us do. Give strengh to those who serve . . . who work towards healing. We pray especially for our doctors, our nurses, our police, our firefighters, our leaders. Let the storms cease . . . calm these seas." Amen. In Jesus' Name. Amen.

JANUARY 14, 2021

I received a really wonderful gift this Christmas. It is a book of conversations between the Dalai Lama and Archbishop Desmond Tutu entitled *The Book of Joy*. First of all . . . the title grabbed me right off!

I need a 'book of joy'. There is so much in life that robs us of our joy. When we begin life we giggle, we laugh, we smile . . . at just about anything. Then our experiences seem to drive some of that joy away.

Remember the first time your child cried a tear? I must be honest to say, I don't. But my wife often tells the story of when she saw that first tear run down our oldest son's face. We don't really remember why the tear came . . . maybe just a moment of discomfort. But we know that as parents we would do just about anything to keep our child from experiencing sadness and losing that sense of joy.

God, our Father really wants us to find that joy in our life. As Jesus made his way to the cross he reminded his followers that even though they would feel sadness, joy would return. In John 16, we read . . . "*Now you are sad, but I will see you again and your hearts will be filled with gladness*".

In *The Book of Joy*, I found these words . . . "We need unbiased love toward entire humanity, entire sentient beings, irrespective of what their attitude is toward us." The conversations went on to discuss the idea that our enemies are still our brothers and sisters and they deserve our love, our respect, our affection.

I love the musical piece, "Ode to Joy". I have heard it played on the stage by excellent orchestras, I have heard many an accomplished organist pound it out! It's an amazing piece. But no more JOY comes to my soul than when my 11 year old granddaughter does a video call with us and plays that favorite selection of mine on her viola. She's only taken lessons for less than a year and I must admit she is no virtuoso! But joy comes to us in so many differerent ways, doesn't it? Sometimes in the very simplest form.

So, find some JOY in your life today. Smile, (we all can see that smile, even behind a mask) laugh, recall a special favorite memory. Let's resolve to experience joy even in these days, in sometimes the most difficult of circumstances.

And, wash your hands. Fold them, bow your heads . . . reflect on the most joyful days of your life. Resolve to share your joy with someone . . . anyone. Plan to get the vaccine when available.

Pray with me: "Dear Lord, sometimes our nights are long and our hearts are heavy. But you have promised us that there will be JOY in the morning. Give us comfort, give us peace. Instill within us the power to share our joy and our love with others. Amen. In Jesus' Name, Amen.

TUESDAY, JANUARY 19, 2021

I am having an awful time with words. Words, like . . . **peace, joy, comfort, love, righteousness, justice, truth, honesty, anger, revenge** . . . some words bring me a sense of calm, some words just seem to 'stick in my craw'!

We play Scrabble sometimes. Actually, quite often these last months. You know how it is, the letters spill out in a jumble and you try to make some sense of them. Try to put them together to make words that are accurate.

Well, that's how I feel today as I make an attempt at sharing a devotional, a 'comforting' thought with you, my friends.

In Matthew 12:37, we read: *"Your words will be used to judge you – to declare you either innocent or guilty."* So, we need to be careful with words. You never really know how others will interpret what we say. Our words can do so much good . . . give comfort, show compassion, inspire. And our words can create havoc. Our words may even be used against us.

It's Martin Luther King Day as I write these thoughts. I have always been inspired to do good in the world by his words. I hope I always am. Our nation and our world is in dire need of a peacemaker right now. Dr. King reminded us . . . *"The arc of the moral universe is long, but it bends toward justice".* Dr. King's words have influenced us for decades. So, words matter. I pray that these words from the Old Testament in Amos still ring true today: *"But let justice roll down like waters, and righteousness like an ever flowing stream."*

Wear a mask. Wash your hands. Fold them, bow your head.

Ask God to help you to be a Peacemaker in our world this day. And please get the vacination when you have the chance. Do it for all of us.

Pray with me: "Dear Lord, we are reminded to choose our words very carefully. Let what we say be an expression of what is in our heart. We are in great need of healing here in this place we inhabit. We pray for peace this week as our nation moves on in the democratic process. Bless us all and God Bless our healers, our workers, our leaders, our troops and the United States of America. Amen. **In Jesus' Name, Amen.**

TUESDAY, JANUARY 26, 2021

I spoke with someone last week who was quite ill with the Covid virus. He told me how disconcerting it was for him when he realized he had lost his sense of taste and smell. He said it didn't come on 'all of a sudden' but gradually he realized he couldn't taste what he was eating and he had no sense of smell.

That got me thinking about the five senses. I love to eat! I just love food . . . and I am known to savor the aroma of what I am about to eat. My wife has been experimenting with baking bread (like many folks during our stay at home experience). I can pull my car into our garage and immediately think to myself . . . "Oh, that smells so good!" I cannot imagine being without any of my senses. It must be quite difficult.

We have a good, old friend who lost his sight many years ago. He had been an air traffic controller, loved to read, loved good wine and good music. He also was a bass fiddle player and it gave him so much comfort to pluck away on that big bass. He didn't have his sight, but his sense of touch became more and more honed. Dick approached life with such vigor and enthusiasm. He was a true visionary.

I'm thinking especially this day about the sense of sight. In Acts 2, we read: *"Your young men will see visions, and your old men will dream dreams."* My sight isn't what it used to be. Most of us are experiencing something similar. So perhaps this is the time for us to encourage our young to see visions . . . to see the present and the future . . . . as we dream our dreams. This quote attributed to Helen Keller is so profound: **"Worse than being blind, is having sight but no vision."**

So this day I hope all of us look around and see what we can see . . . There's an old song that goes like this . . . *"Look out your window, see what you can see. Silence is broken by opening your door. Look out your window, see if you can see . . . all the wonders of life, you've never seen before."*

Just a 'glimpse' of positive thinking for this new week! Wear your mask everywhere, wash your hands, fold them . . . bow your head. Thank God for sight . . . for vision . . . for the beautiful world, just outside our window.

Pray with me: "Dear Lord, you have given us eyes to see. Help us to see what is good, and to go about your work in this world. And give us vision to dream our dreams. Amen. In Jesus' Name, Amen.

THURSDAY, JANUARY 21, 2021

There's an old saying that I learned early in life when I would face a certain disappointment or defeat. It went like this . . . "Get back up, dust yourself off, and start all over again."

I can't help but feel that way this day. We are still going through some tough times with the virus, in our nation and in our world. But maybe this is the time to pick ourselves up . . . dust ourselves off . . . and make a new start.

New starts happened often in the Bible. In Isaiah we find these words . . . *"Watch for the new thing that I am going to do. It is happening already – you can see it now! I will make a road through the wilderness and give you streams of water there."*

So . . . as we pass through these present times and go down new roads I find myself praying hard and heavy for discord, disagreements, discontent to not follow with us down these new paths.

How can we make that happen? Those new streams of water can bring a kind of cleansing. It's all about opening our hearts and our souls to a new understanding. We don't have to keep going down roads tangled with thorns . . . there are new roads out there. And if we follow the lead revealed to us through Scripture, we WILL find a way.

I had a small surgery recently. It created a big, ugly scar! And on my nose, no less! I would check it every morning to see if it looked any better. It's taken a long time . . . but finally, it's not the first thing I notice about myself when I look in the mirror each morning. It's been a steady process of healing. For sure, that scar will probably be there forever, especially at this age! Healing is a difficult process, most times. And it often leaves scars. But if we persevere . . . we do heal.

Let healing begin. Wear a mask. Wash your hands, fold them and bow your head. Get the vaccine as soon as you can . . . do it for all of us. Pray to God that we will heal. Then . . . 'get up, dust yourself off, and start all over again!"

Pray with me: "Dear Lord, we pray for healing in our nation. We pray for healing from this horrible virus. We pray for strength to get down difficult paths. And we pray for our leaders, our healers, our protectors and ourselves. Give us strength to begin again." Amen.

In Jesus' Name, Amen.

THURSDAY, JANUARY 28, 2021

I find myself spending a little more time thinking about our senses . . . sight, smell, sound, touch and taste.

After speaking with someone who had lost his sense of smell during a bout with the coronavirus I was reminded of what a pleasure it is to smell something wonderful. Fresh baked bread! For sure . . . but before I sat down to write this I took a step outside. It rained! Something that is worth a celebration here in Southern Arizona! There is just nothing like the smell of the moist ground after a good rain.

So . . . I found myself happy to 'see' the raindrops on the cactus, and to 'smell' the earth's excitement over that moisture.

Not long after my mother died I remember being in Dayton's in Fargo, ND. In a brief moment I felt my breath taken away. I could smell her! Well, it was just some other lovely lady who was standing at my side . . . she was wearing the perfume my mother wore most of her life. She would get a bottle from my dad for her birthday and Christmas every year. It wasn't expensive, I am sure. But it was her 'scent'. And to this very day . . . I can identify it.

In II Corinthians 2:15 we read, *"For we are like a sweet smelling incense offered by Christ to God, which spreads among those who are being saved and those who are being lost."* We are God's FRAGRANCE in the world. What a beautiful thought!

When we sense a wonderful aroma spread around us, it's quite pleasant, isn't it? That is what we can be for our world. Not Stinkers! But 'Aroma Spreaders'! Think about that today.

It's rather easy to spread our stinking thoughts but it might take a little more effort to spread that sweet perfume that God has given us to put to good use.

I'm stuck on figuring out how to use my 'good senses' in better ways. In the meantime, wear a mask. Fold your hands, bow your heads and ask God for ways to spread that sweet perfume around everywhere. And please get that vaccine when you can. Do it for all of us.

Pray with me: "Dear Lord, You have given us so many ways to be about your mission. Inspire us to cleanse our thoughts and our hearts. We can be so stinking rotten sometimes . . . give us strength to do your good work. Amen. In Jesus' Name, Amen.

FEBRUARY 2, 2021

I am reflecting on our five senses as I write these devotional thoughts. I have to say, 'sight' and 'smell' were interesting. And NOW . . . I'm thinking about 'taste'.

As I have mentioned before, food is a powerful thing for me. I remember my grandmother . . . when she made a meal and everyone would exclaim and exclaim about how delicious all the food was, her response always went like this . . . *"dette smaker ikke sa godt"*. In other words, "it's really not as good as it should be". The dear woman just couldn't take a compliment . . . it wasn't in her 'Norwegian' makeup.

But it **was** wonderful! All those old Scandinavian delicacies were her specialty. The taste comes back to me when I close my eyes and dwell on . . . potato sausage, warm lefse with sugar, right off the grill, and of course . . . lutefisk.

(Well, we have heard it said . . . "One person's passion may be another's poison!")

In Psalm 34:8, we read . . . *"Taste and see that the Lord is Good"*. And just how do we 'taste' the Lord? There are various thoughts on that, but I like to think about our sense of taste as we share in the Lord's Supper. When those words are said over the elements we share . . . *"This is the body of Christ . . . this is the blood of Christ"*, we have the opportunity to taste the goodness of our Lord. It is a holy moment as we share in His very body and blood, not only with one another, but with the angels and the archangels who surround us.

So, when I share in the Holy Communion with you, as we

have the opportunity to do through our online worship experience, I often close my eyes and feel the presence of my grandparents, my parents and those who have gone before me. The angels and the archangels, who are cheering me on through this life.

And I often hear in my mind my beloved grandmother saying . . . *"Maten smaker godt!"*. "That tasted good." And it does. It is the best of all the tastes there are.

Join with me as a Family of God, sharing that Good Meal . . . "Taste and see that the Lord is good".

Wear a mask . . . or two, keep washing your hands, fold them and bow you head. Thank God for the chance to taste and see how good God really is.

Pray with me: "Dear Lord, thank you for coming to us in the bread and the wine. So often we need a real reminder of how good you really are. There are days when we search for your presence and then . . . there you are. Right in front of us in the simplest of elements. We give you thanks for that. Strengthen us in our journey and give us insight to see the right road to travel. Amen. In Jesus' Name, Amen.

Many times throughout the Gospels Jesus uses these words . . . *"He who has ears, let him hear."*

Hearing is an amazing gift. As many of you can identify, my hearing isn't what it used to be. I know that's just something that comes with aging. And then there are those times when I hear (in a loud voice) . . . **Do you HEAR me?** Yes, that happens.

So . . . maybe it isn't so much about 'hearing', as it is about 'listening'. Jesus is clearly telling us that we have the capacity to HEAR Him. But we may not be listening.

In James 1:19, we read, *"Everyone must be quick to listen, but slow to speak and slow to become angry."*

Quick . . . to listen. I suppose that means turning one's attention away from the television or the book one is concentrating on so steadily . . . tuning out all the clamor around us and really 'listening', focusing on the speaker. Ever find yourself so distracted when 'listening' to someone that when they finish speaking and look at you with that quizzical look . . . you have no idea what just was said? That's been my experience more than once.

I remember when the children were small and on more than one occasion they would take my face in their little hands and say . . . face to face . . . LISTEN TO ME! As I look back on that, I wish I would have been more 'quick to listen'. Slower to speak and slower to become angry.

We can certainly apply those words to our living in these days. We may 'hear' certain things and then go about repeating or disparaging what we have heard, when in truth . . . we really didn't 'listen' very carefully.

And then there is that anger. It often does come after some 'not so careful' listening and too quickly speaking. So, let's all focus on becoming better listeners. Really listening. And then, maybe holding our tongue. If we do that, the level of anger might just go down a notch or two. I hope so.

Wear your mask, wash your hands, fold them, bow your head and ask God to give you the ability to be a better listener. I know I need to work on that.

Pray with me: "Dear Lord, so many times we find ourselves angry because we have spoken before we really 'heard' what was said. Help us to listen more and speak less. We pray especially for those good listeners who sit at the bedside of the sick, for those who listen to the cries of the depressed, for those who listen for the whole story before making judgements. Give us all a little more patience to really listen. Amen. In Jesus' Name, Amen.

FEBRUARY 9, 2021

One of the many comments I have heard during this time of isolation due to the Coronavirus is . . . "I miss hugging people . . . I don't even shake hands with anyone". Especially for those who live alone, this has been so very difficult.

The sense of 'Touch'. It's essential. We need to touch one another. It's not about intimacy, but more the idea that we are 'in touch' with one another.

Jesus did it the best. When we read in John 13 about the Passover Meal we can visualize that scene . . . *"Then he poured some water into a washbasin and began to wash the disciples' feet and dry them with the towel that was around his waist."* Jesus KNEW that his friends, his disciples, would need to remember his touch during the difficult days ahead.

Virus or no virus, when we have the chance to see our grandchildren once again I guarantee you that I will envelop them with the biggest hug I can give! I need to TOUCH those little people. I need to FEEL them in my arms.

Sometimes love feels very 'abstract', doesn' it? We feel that we are so far away from one another. Some folks feel as though they will never experience the touch of another again. So . . . we remember. Just as the disciples, the friends, of Jesus were left with the memory of his touch. His hands washing their dirty feet. His arms wrapping a towel around them. It was a beautiful thing Jesus did.

We are also left with the memory of touch. Ever feel touched by the Spirit of God? Most certainly you have, as have I. Sometimes we keep those thoughts secured in our souls and when we need to remember a certain 'touch', they come back to us.

It is so important for us all to remember that this 'touch' of God is upon our hearts and our souls each and every moment. As we rise in the mornings we recall the words of our Baptism . . . being touched with the water and being named as God's child. One day soon we will surely be able to hug, to shake hands, to 'high five' . . . to touch one another.

But for now . . . wash your hands. Fold them and see your thumbs in the shape of that cross, bow your head and give thanks. Give thanks for the water, the washing away, the Word and God's loving touch.

Pray with me: "Dear Lord, in our alone times, in our lonely hours, we give thanks that You are right there with us. Washing us, wrapping us in your love. Help us to reach out to one another – the sad, the lonely, the afraid, the poor, the hungry. We are your 'touch' in this frightened world. Amen. In Jesus' Name, Amen.

THURSDAY, FEBRUARY 11, 2021

As I mentioned earlier, I have been reading *The Book of Joy*, conversations between the Dali Lama and Bishop Tutu. I have found myself stuck on one certain conversation the two gentlemen had about FORGIVENESS.

We all know that sometimes it is easier to forgive than to forget. Although, if we truly 'forgive' . . . can it be 'forgiveness' if we never 'forget'?

The Bible is full of passages concerning forgiveness. I like the one in Colossian 3 . . . *"Be tolerant with one another and forgive one another"*.

Forgiveness may not come easily . . . but tolerance? That's another story! I find as I age, I am less and less tolerant. Of a lot of things. That's something to work on.

In *The Book of Joy* I read . . . *"There are those who think an eye for an eye is going to satisfy. But in the end you discover that an eye for an eye will leave the whole world blind."*

When we have been wronged, especially by those close to us, forgiveness is difficult. I have struggled with forgiveness myself. I still find that when I think of things that happened in my father's family I harbor that feeling of resentment so I wonder if my forgiveness has been true. Maybe that's where the forgetting part comes in.

Jesus knew all about forgiveness. Remember his words . . . ***"Father, forgive them for they know not what they do"***. As we begin our Lenten walk next week with Ash Wednesday, I am going to try to remember . . . remember those times when forgiveness did not come easily. And then I am going to work on FORGETTING. Because maybe sometimes when we felt we have been wronged . . . 'they did not even know what they were doing'. It's something to think about.

And be tolerant. Wear a mask, wash your hands and fold them. Bow your head, ask God for forgiveness. Forgive one another. And then work on forgetting.

Pray with me: "Dear Lord, increase within us a desire to forgive. And also help us to be more tolerant. Tolerant of those we are so close to and those we feel distance from. Remind us daily to open our blinded eyes to see the other side. Amen. In Jesus' Name, Amen.

We have been spending some of our 'covid time' going through our many possessions. There are some things that we have carted around with us for far too long. Like our high school and college annuals. Those books are big! And we have moved them many times. I can't imagine that when we are no longer on this earth our children 'pouring' over them with such gratitude that we had saved them.

So what to do with such things? It really makes us realize what is important to us and what doesn't matter so much.

We all know what the Bible has to say . . . just start reading in Matthew and you will have clear direction . . . *"What does it profit a man if he gains the whole world but loses his soul?"* And it does go on and on . . . . *"Do not store up for yourself riches here on earth"* . . . . etc., etc.

I wouldn't really call our old annuals 'riches here on earth', but it has made me realize that I have spent a great deal of my life acquiring things that now I need to figure out where they should go. Ironic, isn't it? It's kind of a soul searching as we begin to think about what it is that really is important in our lives.

In my first parish I came to know a very wise old guy. His name was Sigval. He probably had more money than many of those Red River Valley farmers, but his house was nothing more than a shack. He had a few pieces of furniture, very simply decorated. But his wealth was really in his view of life. When we would visit I would go from that farmstead filled with perspective. He had a way of helping me to zero in on the important matters of life. He had a deep, deep soul. So when I reflect on those words . . . *"What does it profit a man if he gains the whole world but loses his soul"* . . . I think of Sigval. He helped me put those words in perspective.

Not to say things aren't important. They certainly are, and they give us a great deal of pleasure. Sometimes we just need to do a little 'house cleaning' . . . a 'soul searching' to keep us focused on what really matters.

Wash you hands. Fold them and bow your head. Pray for direction to keep focused on the really important things. And please, if you have not already done so . . . get the vaccine. Don't just do it for yourself, do it for all of us.

Pray with me: "Dear Lord, help us not to be so focused on what it is that we need every day. Help us to see the bigger picture. Give us faith to find pleasure in the simple things in life. Keep us focused. Amen. In Jesus' Name, Amen.

FEBRUARY 18, 2021

"Remember, you are dust and to dust you shall return."

Those ashes placed on our forehead this year have prompted me to think of the near 600,000-plus lives we have lost to this pandemic. 600,000 families whose lives have been changed forever.

A year ago we began this journey together. We struggled with how to do church services, Easter Celebrations, etc. and in my mind . . . I KNEW this was just a short time in our lives. The pandemic would soon be behind us and we would return to 'normal'.

And here we are. A year has gone by and we still find ourselves doing things differently than we have ever done before.

It's just plain sobering. So we come to terms once more that we are really nothing but dust. We come and we go. It is the life we live as we move from dust to dust that really matters. It is in the days we spend caring for one another. Loving one another. Showing respect for one another. All people. All folks – with no regard for race, color or religion.

I don't want to be remembered as JUST DUST! I want my family, my friends, my fellow church members, my neighbors to see me as more than that. And how do we make that happen?

These are the times that call us out to be what Jesus Christ, the one who walked the way to Gethsemane, the one who hung upon that cross . . . charged us as His namesakes to be. We are to be more than dust . . . we are to be the salt of the earth. The light of this world.

So I ask you to take this Lenten Walk with me as we move from dust to dust . . . let's be a little more salty! Let's let that light shine a bit brighter! It's not good enough to just keep on keeping on. It's time to do what God calls us to do in this world. For our world is not a dismal place. It is a place of hope, it is a time for determination. It is a time for us to build one another up and then . . . carry on.

In the meantime, it is so important for us to wear our masks, to get our shots, keep washing our hands. To fold those hands and bow our heads. It is time for us to ask God to help us be salt and light.

Pray with me: "Dear Lord, we cannot just accept that the world is a difficult place. We need you to imspire and direct us as to how we can change it. We pray especially for those who are so tired of taking care of others. Give them your strength. We walk now with you to the cross these weeks. We have come from the dust and it is to the dust we will return. But in the meantime, let us be your hands and feet in this world today. Amen. In Jesus' Name, Amen."

TUESDAY, FEBRUARY 23, 2021

You may recall the devotion I wrote last week about doing a little 'soul searching'. I was inspired by the many comments I received from folks about that. It appears that soul searching is something with which we all can identify.

One person said . . . "Interesting what you find when you climb into your head". Wow! I really like that.

So . . . . I did that. I spent a little time 'climbing into my head'. It was amazing what I found. Some stuff in there that I'm not so proud of. Some stuff I thought I was completely past.

The Bible tells us in I Corinthians 3:16, *"Do you not know that you are God's temple and that God's Spirit dwells in you?"*

Wouldn't it be something when we find ourselves delving deep inside where we really live, we find the Spirit of God? That Spirit lives in us, you know. Sometimes I am so disappointed with myself when I 'do the things I would not do, and do not do the things I would'. It is at those times that I need to remember that the Spirit of the Living God is really, truly deep inside of me.

That takes me to Romans 15:2 . . . *"Instead, we should all please our brothers for their own good, in order to build them up in the faith"*. Climbing inside our heads and discovering that we are a living, breathing messenger of God's Spirit can take us to another place. A place where we discover that we can put that Spirit to work in how we live and how we care for one another.

Just a bit of 'musing' on those thoughts about soul searching. I'm planning on doing some more of it. Hope you are, too.

And thanks so much for sharing your words with me about these devotional thoughts. YOU are doing your part 'building others up in the the faith'.

Keep on washing your hands, fold them, bow your head. Search your soul . . . you will find the Spirit of the Living God there.

Pray with me: "Dear Lord, help us to find that inner self. The place where we know your Spirit lives. Encouraging us, uplifing us and inspiring us. And also, help us to do more to help one another. To build each other up. Amen. In Jesus' Name, Amen."

THURSDAY, FEBRUARY 25, 2021

As I mentioned a few devotionals back, we have been doing a bit of sorting through things. As I was going through some old photos recently I came across some pictures of my grandfather and my grandmother. They were Norwegian emmigrants who settled in central North Dakota.

The photos were of the home farm where my father and eventually, myself and my siblings grew up. These were some of the very first photos ever taken of that farmsite. After my parents died we made the hard decision to sell the land and this farmsite. Last summer on a trip back to North Dakota we decided to drive by the farm, which we knew was now deserted. As I drove into the old driveway, overridden with grass, I was shocked to see the farmhouse gone. It had burned down and very little remained.

There was so much history in that place. Of course, I was sad but then I noticed some new trees had sprouted up where the driveway used to be. I saw some growth there . . . and maybe, possibilities for a new home, sheltered by the trees my father and grandfather had planted.

In Isaiah 43:19, we read . . . *"Behold, I will do a new thing; now it shall spring forth . . . I will even make a way in the wilderness, and rivers in the desert."*

There are times in life when the 'old things' just don't work any longer. And we need to see a 'new thing'. I think particularly of family and friends who have found that the time comes for a new adventure. Some of those decisions are very difficut and some come easily. But Isaiah is so filled with hope in times of change. It always gives me courage to read those words. Hopefully, for you too.

As we move through these months of change as a church we need to focus on those profound words of Isaiah . . . "*Behold, I will do a new thing!*" NEW isn't always easy, it isn't always fun but it can be renewing, refreshing and a time for spiritual growth. Read on in Isaiah . . . as we make our way.

And please, keep on washing your hands. Fold them, bow your heads and ask God for direction. If you have not had your vaccinations I urge you to get them. I am fortunate to have had my second shot and am excited to begin worshipping with you in person this weekend. Please wear your masks. For all of us.

Pray with me: "Dear Lord, we are so timid when it comes to new things. We like things to stay the way they were. But sometimes change just happens. Help us to face our future with courage as you direct our ways. Amen. In Jesus' Name, Amen."

TUESDAY, MARCH 2, 2021

Jesus did a lot of things on his way to the cross. He brought together his disciples. He calmed some storms, He told some stories . . . and He healed a few folks.

I think that's pretty exciting! The healings, I mean. He healed a man with a dreaded skin disease, He touched Peter's mother-in-law who had a fever, and the fever left her. He healed two men with demons and a paralyzed man. He healed some blind men and a man with the inability to speak.

And then . . . in Matthew 9, he tells his followers . . . *"Jesus spoke sternly to those whom he had healed . . .* **'DON'T TELL THIS TO ANYONE'***!"*

What was that about? Reminds me of my growing up days. If I excelled at anything my parents would always remind me . . . "You don't need to go about bragging". We were taught to keep quiet about our accomplishments! Must have been the Scandinavian in us.

Why would Jesus tell people not to brag about what he had done? I can't help but wonder if he knew that the physical healings he performed would certainly play out in the arena much more powerfully than the spiritual message he wished to send. It kind of goes back to the message I was thinking about last week . . . but in this case, Jesus' words spoke more than his actions.

Or . . . maybe Jesus just didn't want the focus to be so much on him, and more on the message. I remember years ago hearing the story of Billy Graham. Rev. Graham was being celebrated for his dedication to ministry at an event. People were giving talks about the wonderful things he had accomplished and finally it came time for him to take the stage. I've never forgotten the words he shared . . . "I think this is just way too much about Billy Graham and not enough about Jesus."

I think in this message from Matthew Jesus is reminding us that we need not focus on the "ME" or the "I" so much and turn our minds and our hearts to the message He carried on this earth and all the way to the cross.

And, wear your mask . . . wash your hands, fold them and bow your head. Thank God for helping us to see the importance of living through Lent.

Pray with me: "Dear Lord, remind me often that your mission is not about me . . . it is about You. Give strength to the weary, peace to the stressed, calm to the anxious and love to the broken hearted. Amen. In Jesus' Name, Amen.

THURSDAY, MARCH 4, 2021

As I am going with you through these days of Lent it is so interesting to read through all the things that happened with Jesus and the disciples on the way to the cross. He knew where he was going, I'm not so sure very many of them had a clue.

I like the story of James and John as it is told in Mark. Years ago we had friends who had twin sons they named James and John. Whenever I think about those boys I think of the story in Mark.

Jesus had been telling the disciples what was about to happen. As they listened, James and John asked Jesus if they could be the ones who would sit on his right and on his left as he came into the kingdom. I remember those boys I knew years ago . . . it seemed like they were true to their names and were always presuring their dad about who was the favorite. They were good kids but they knew how to 'press their dad's buttons'.

Jesus listens to the two and then he tells them in no uncertain terms that it's just not his call. Read on in Mark and you will get to the part where he says . . . *"If one of you wants to be great, he must be the servant of the rest, he must be the slave to all . . . for even the Son of Man did not come to be served, He came to serve and to give his life to redeem many people."*

Isn't this a good reminder as we continue our way to the cross? It's all about servanthood . . . giving up for the good of all. We really don't need to be the 'favorite' one. We don't even need the 'first place' at the table. Jesus reminds us over and over again that we are to be servants. A servant church. Seeking out where we can do more for others.

It's a Lenten theme. Not so much about the royalty, the throne, the crown . . . but about the cross, the wreath of thorns, the sacrifice. We'll get to the "Alleluias!", the "Crown Him with Many Crowns" . . . but first we need to walk the walk, step by step. Making our way, just as he did.

Remember to keep washing your hands, fold them, study your thumbs in the shape of that cross, bow your heads and make room in your heart for the serving Christ. And please wear a mask . . . for all of us.

Pray with me: "Dear Lord, so often we worry about where our place at the table is. And then we hear your words of being a slave to all. Open our hearts and our minds to not be so critical of one another. Help us walk the walk . . . step by step. Amen, In Jesus' Name, Amen."

There are so many times that I found the words of Isaiah in chapter 40 comforting . . . *"But those who trust in the Lord for help will find their strength renewed. They will rise up on wings like eagles, they will run and not get weary; they will walk and not grow weak."*

It is a passage that has strengthened many of you, as well, I am certain. It came to my mind this past week when I thought about a friend we have had for many years. As a young woman she became very sick and had to have a surgery to correct an issue. She has lived with physical pain and discomfort since that time and yet has raised her family, worked in her profession and been an inspiration to her many friends.

This past week in a conversation with my wife she shared how sick she had become following her second vaccination. Many folks have suffered the same discomfort. But she said quite plainly . . . "I've been through worse! I'll be just fine!" And my wife responded . . . "You are a survivor!"

What does it take to be a survivor when life can be so hard? Determination? Courage? Strength? I'm not so sure and I am certain our friend would agree. There are times in life when it is so difficult and we don't feel so determined . . . or courageous . . . or strong. What do we do then?

For me, those words of Isaiah just seem to pop into my mind. We trust . . . and often we do find our strength renewed. And we look ahead to the days when we run, and not get weary. When we can walk, and not grow weak.

As I have conversation with so many of you I gain my strength by your shared stories. So, when you do feel weary and wonder just HOW you will survive, look to Isaiah. I know how difficult some of these days are and I hold you in my prayers and in my heart. Take courage from the words . . . *"You WILL rise up on wings like eagles, you WILL run and not get weary, you WILL walk and not grow weak."*

And remember to keep on washing your hands, fold them in prayer. Bow you head and ask God for that strength that lifts the eagle's wings.

Pray with me: "Dear Lord, our hearts are heavy with those we love who struggle with physical pain, lonliness, sadness. Help us to offer the strength you give. Let us be the wind that lifts those who falter. Bind us together as your servants in the world. Amen, In Jesus' Name, Amen.

THURSDAY, MARCH 11, 2021

I am enjoying reading a book called, *Dakota Attitude.* It was a gift from fellow North Dakotans and it is a compilation of many interviews from every town/city in the state of North Dakota. It's amazing how many of the names I recognize! Maybe what they say is true . . . "If you are from North Dakota, chances are you know someone in almost every town!" Maybe it's because there just weren't that many of us.

In any case, some of the stories are heart warming and some are heart wrenching. Most tell the tales of growing up on a farm or in a small town and having to work hard to get through life. Most of these folks remained in those towns and were the building blocks of what it took to keep their hometowns alive.

It makes me think of the saying . . . "Never forget where you came from". In Jesus's day they said it this way . . . "What good can come out of Nazareth?" So there he was . . . a carpenter's son from a not so fancy town. And to this very day, we are walking the way He walked. To the cross.

Jesus had the knack of knowing where He came from. He never forgot that his life was a simple one. I think that's why he identified so well with the common folks. Have you ever met someone very strong and powerful? Been amazed at the fact that you could even shake the hand of such a person? I remember one experience I had many years ago. My parents and I went to see a person running for public office. He was very popular and everyone wanted to shake his hand. I stood back, intimidated, for sure. He happened to catch my eye and walked right over to me and introduced himself. We shook hands and it was a moment I will never forget. That gentleman was President John Kennedy.

To walk the Lenten Walk with Jesus is to be in the presence of the most powerful person ever to land his feet upon our earth. He reaches out to each and every one of us on this walk. He invites us to accompany him. And soon we will reach the foot of the cross and once again, we will be amazed at the sight of this one man . . . giving up ALL for such simple folks as you and I.

Keep on washing your hands, fold them and look upon your thumbs in the shape of that cross, bow your head and give thanks for remembering from where we have come . . . and where we are headed. Please share the Lenten Worship Services with Pastor Dennis Nelson as he leads the way.

Pray with me: "Dear Lord, I know where I came from . . . and I know where I am going. Thank you for leading me, directing me and helping me every step of the way. Help me to share this way with those who struggle. Amen. In Jesus' Name, Amen.

For some reason I have been thinking a lot about RECONCILIA-TION lately. Probably because so many folks have been at odds with one another and that is troubling.

They say sometimes you just 'have to draw a line in the sand'. In other words, this line is drawn and one is on one side of the line . . . and the other, on the opposite side. So, as 'reconcilers' how to we come to an agreement?

The problem often is that no one wants to 'give in' and be the first to step forward. So, the line just stays in place and the two simply cannot meet. Paul reminds us in Ephesians 4:32 that "*Instead, be kind and tender-hearted to one another, and forgive one another as God has forgiven you through Christ.*"

Great words, but it still is going to take the action of that first person to be willing to step up to the line. And forgive. I think about this when I share stories with so many who still struggle with forgiveness. As a 'reconciler' I would just like to give those folks on either side of that line a big PUSH! Step up . . . be the first one. Then there may be that moment when reconciliation takes place and the following steps can be down that line . . . in the same direction.

Sometimes I find myself on the other side of that line. I know how difficult that first move is. And you wonder? Will the other person meet me there? Or will I be rejected in my move for reconciliation?

I guess it takes faith. And forgiveness. And time. And then . . . just be courageous, move forward. Remember those words . . . *"forgive one another, as God has forgiven you through Christ Jesus."*

Keep on wearing your mask. Wash your hands, fold them and bow your head. Ask God for courage to move on. And please get your vaccination whenever you can. Do it for all of us.

Pray with me: "Dear Lord, so often I am so stubborn. I just cannot let go of the past and the wrongs I feel have been done to me. Help me to be strong and take the first step. Amen. In Jesus' Name, Amen."

THURSDAY, MARCH 18, 2021

This past week there have been many stories about grandparents finally being able to hug their grandchildren after receiving the second vaccination. Just a few weeks ago we had the pleasure of meeting our daughter and granddaughter at the airport in Tucson with GREAT BIG HUGS! And at the end of this week we will be standing at the bottom of our driveway with open arms as the other three 'grands' pull up to our very door. We will be ready to HUG!

It's been a long hard time for many people. Those stories of long awaited hugs are beautiful. Maybe you've seen the video of the grandmother and granddaughter who just couldn't seem to let each other go. In Ecclesiastes it even says . . . *"there is a time to scatter stones and a time to gather them; a time to embrace and a time to refrain from embracing."*

Well, time is up for me! Pre-covid when friends would arrive for a meal, or when we would see our extended family, a tight hug was assured! But we haven't done that for a year and thankfully, if we are careful . . . the time to embrace is eminent.

When I reflect on those tight hugs I can't help but find myself thinking of all those 550,000-plus family members who most likely didn't have the moment of that final embrace. This virus has taken it's toll, for sure. And then I also think of those women who visited the empty tomb on Easter morning. Most likely, they didn't have the chance for that final embrace with Jesus. So, they made their way to do the next best thing. They were there to tend to his body. But the tomb was empty! It seemed as though their final act of service was denied.

Shock upon shock! They met who they thought was maybe just a gardener. But it was the Lord. Hugging wasn't an option, but even without that physical touch . . . they felt His love and His presence. We can identify. We have been here for one another in so many varied ways this past year. Just as we cannot feel the physical touch of the Crucified Christ . . . we know, in the bread and the wine . . . His Presence.

And keep on washing your hands, fold them, bow your heads and feel His presence as we walk these final steps to the cross.

Pray with me: "Dear Lord, we are thankful for each and every embrace. For the love of family and good friends who have helped us on our way through these long days. Open our hearts and our minds to the message of Holy Week as we look ahead to the glory of Easter. Amen, In Jesus' Name, Amen."

Ilove the term we hear at Desert Hills often . . . "Laughter Liberates!" It is liberating to laugh, isn't it? In Genesis 21 we read the story of the birth of a boy to Abraham and Sarah. They were old folks. So it was quite a surprise to them when Isaac was to be born. The Bible tells us Sarah said . . . *"God has brought me joy and laughter. Everyone who hears about it will laugh with me."*

I like that she tells us that folks will laugh 'with' her and not 'at' her. It's never a very good thing when we get laughed at! Last week I had an interesting experience. As I was about to enter the church in the morning I had way too much in my hands and I felt myself take a misstep. Of course . . . down I went! No injuries but the first thing I did was to look around and make sure no one saw me. No luck there! Not in this place. Of course, my stumble was noticed! But we all just laughed. Not 'at' me . . . but 'with' me.

Sometimes we just have to do a better job at laughing at ourselves. Or maybe, just a better job at laughing. It is liberating. During Lent things get a bit somber, we are walking to the cross, of course. It was a hard time for Jesus and his friends. Hard times can really get you down. Laughter and tears are freqently so connected. I remember when my mother-in-law died and my wife and her sisters were telling funny stories about their mom. Even though we all were in a rather dark place, we found ourselves laughing and laughing . . . through the tears.

We know that joy comes in the morning. There are smiles and laughter after tears. It's the last few steps now and we can feel consumed with our sadness. We will meet our Lord this Sunday with palms and hallelujahs. Then we will suffer through those last days. But Easter will come! After tears . . . . songs of joy.

Keep on washing your hands. Fold them, bow your head and pray for sunshine after rain. Laughter following tears. And please, get your vaccination. It's the wise thing to do. I really believe that.

Pray with me: "Dear Lord, you brought joy and laughter to Abraham and Sarah. Keep us focused on what lies ahead as we welcome Him with palms and cheers . . . and then tears. Give us strength for what lies ahead. Amen. In Jesus' name, Amen."

TUESDAY, MARCH 30, 2021

Here we are . . . Holy Week. We worshipped on Palm Sunday, welcoming the King of Kings with palm branches and calls of 'Hosanna'. But we all knew what was ahead for us . . . and for Jesus.

It's very exciting to welcome someone. Recently we had two separate visits from family. We could hardly wait for them to arrive! But before we knew it, they were gone. The house seemed very empty without the sounds of young people laughing, some dog barking and the conversations we enjoyed so much.

We knew that day would come and they would be gone. It's an empty feeling, isn't it? But we also know that there are good times ahead and we will be together again very soon.

The followers of Jesus didn't quite understand that concept. They welcomed Him with shouts and cheers. But before they knew it, He was gone. He was to die. They thought He was gone forever.

John 16:16 puts it this way: ***"In a little while, you will see me no more, and then after a little while you will see me."*** The people didn't know quite what to make of those words. When they saw Jesus hanging on the cross they thought . . . "Well. That's it." He is gone forever.

That's the beauty of the Easter message. He is not gone. He is with us today as we walk through this week and He is with us as we journey through all our sorrows, our disappointments and our sadness. "A little while" can be just a fleeting moment or it can be longer than we would like it to be. But at the end of 'a little while' comes a grand reunion with laughter, cheers and joy.

Take time these days of Holy Week to reflect on that

thought. And please, keep on washing your hands, fold them and bow your head. This long week ends with an empty tomb and the songs of Alleluia! He is Risen! (It's just 'a little while'.)

Pray with me: "Dear Lord, you reminded us that time is not of the essence where you are. You have not left us and you never will. You walk beside us each and every day. Give us courage to just keep putting one foot in front of the other as we keep on. We are broken hearted at your suffering but we know that it was . . . 'just a little while'. Amen. In Jesus' Name, Amen."

THURSDAY, APRIL 1, 2021

It's been quite a year! I have been sharing these thoughts with you for the past year as we have all struggled with the effects of the Coronavirus. We've had our 'ups and downs' this past year, that is for sure.

This will be my final thought for these days. There always has to be a 'beginning' and an 'end', doesn't there?

So . . . I opened my Bible to Genesis 1:1, *"In the beginning . . . God created the universe"*. It all started with God. God was with us in the very beginning. As I sat to write the first devotional thought a year ago I wondered what I could possibly share that would lighten the load of this journey. I just decided that if I could remind myself and all of us that God is there for us every step of the way . . . that would be sufficient. And He has been.

I will soon close 50-plus years of pastoral ministry. It has taken our family to many places and through many experiences. But once again . . . our God has led us and sustained us. Don't think there haven't been times of questioning . . . we all have those thoughts. But we do not walk this walk alone.

And the Bible ends with Revelation 22:20-21: **"He who gives his testimony to all this says, 'Yes Indeed! I am coming soon! So be it. Come, Lord Jesus! May the grace of the Lord Jesus be with you now and forever."**

I thank you for reading these many messages, for your kind words of encouragement and for the love of God you have shared with one another and with me. And I urge you to get the vaccination, do it for all of us. Don't forget to keep on washing your hands, fold them and look down upon your thumbs in the shape of that cross. Bow your head and give thanks for the Risen Lord Jesus Christ who we will celebrate this Easter Morn. Thank you again for your love and for your prayers.

Pray with me: "Dear Lord, you have blessed our lives beyond measure. You have given us many friends and family who have walked the walk right along side of us. Give strength to the weary, food for the hungry, comfort for the broken-hearted and faith to those who falter. Our lives are full . . . To God be the Glory!" Amen. In Jesus' Name, Amen.

And now may the peace that passes all understanding guard your hearts and your minds through Christ Jesus, our Lord. AMEN.

CPSIA information can be obtained
at www.ICGtesting.com
Printed in the USA
FSHW012309100821